Perpetual Motion

Creative Movement Exercises for Dance and Dramatic Arts

Janice Pomer

Human Kinetics

Library of Congress Cataloging-in-Publication Data

Pomer, Janice, 1955-
    Perpetual motion : creative movement exercises for dance and dramatic arts / Janice Pomer.
      p. cm
    ISBN 0-7360-3393-9
      1. Movement education. 2. Dance--Study and teaching. 3. Drama--Study and teaching.
    I. Title.

    GV452 .P66 2002
    792.8'071--dc21

                                                                                        2001039805

ISBN: 0-7360-3393-9

Acquisitions Editor: Judy Patterson Wright, PhD; **Managing Editor:** Amy Stahl; **Assistant Editor:** Derek Campbell; **Copyeditor:** Barbara Walsh; **Proofreader:** Joanna Hatzopoulos Portman; **Graphic Designer:** Fred Starbird; **Graphic Artist:** Tara Welsch; **Photo Managers:** Les Woodrum, Clark Brooks; **Cover Designer:** Jack W. Davis; **Photographer (cover):** Janice Pomer; **Photographers (interior):** Author photo and photo on p. 148 by Barry Prophet. All other photos by Janice Pomer; **Art Managers:** Craig Newsom, Carl Johnson; **Illustrator:** Dick Flood; **Printer:** Versa Press

Printed in the United States of America

10 9 8 7 6 5 4 3 2 1

Human Kinetics
Web site: www.humankinetics.com

United States: Human Kinetics
P.O. Box 5076
Champaign, IL 61825-5076
800-747-4457
e-mail: humank@hkusa.com

Canada: Human Kinetics
475 Devonshire Road Unit 100
Windsor, ON N8Y 2L5
800-465-7301 (in Canada only)
e-mail: orders@hkcanada.com

Europe: Human Kinetics
Units C2/C3 Wira Business Park
West Park Ring Road
Leeds LS16 6EB, United Kingdom
+44 (0) 113 278 1708
e-mail: hk@hkeurope.com

Australia: Human Kinetics
57A Price Avenue
Lower Mitcham, South Australia 5062
08 8277 1555
e-mail: liahka@senet.com.au

New Zealand: Human Kinetics
P.O. Box 105-231, Auckland Central
09-523-3462
e-mail: hkp@ihug.co.nz

To all my students—past, present, and future.

Contents

Chapter 1 Rules   1

The Concept Behind Rules   1

Application   2

Chapter 2 Recipes   37

The Concept Behind Recipes   37

Application   38

Chapter 3 Props   61

Chapter 4 Poetry and Prose   *83*

Chapter 5 Objects and Images   *111*

Chapter 6 Dancescape Projects   135

Learning Skills Reference Chart

	Page Number	Focus and Concentration	Listening Skills	Language Skills	Internal Rhythm	Problem-Solving Skills	Spatial Awareness	Group Dynamics	Technical Movement Skills	Performance Skills	Personal Aesthetics	Leadership	Analyze and Translate Information Into Movement
Chapter 1 – Rules													
Back to Front	3	✓				✓	✓	✓					
Five Times Five	7	✓				✓	✓				✓		
Wave Walk	10	✓	✓			✓	✓	✓					
Tag	14	✓				✓				✓	✓		
Walk on the Wild Side	17	✓				✓	✓	✓					
Mirrors	20	✓					✓	✓	✓				✓	
Flocking	23	✓				✓		✓	✓				✓	
Ping-Pong	26	✓				✓				✓			✓	
Is the Hand Faster Than the Eye?	28	✓	✓			✓								
Isolation Conversations	30	✓	✓			✓								
Body Parts	32	✓				✓	✓					✓		
Add Water and Stir	34	✓	✓			✓			✓		✓			
Chapter 2 – Recipes													
Recipes for Novice Dancers: Solos	39					✓			✓	✓	✓			✓
Recipes for Novice Dancers: Ensembles	43					✓		✓	✓	✓	✓		✓	✓
Recipes for Elementary- and Intermediate-Level Dancers: Solos	47					✓			✓	✓	✓		✓	✓
Recipe for Elementary- and Intermediate-Level Dancers: Ensemble	51					✓		✓	✓	✓	✓		✓	✓
Recipe Exploring Dramatic Potential of Movement and Voice	53					✓		✓	✓	✓	✓		✓	✓
Recipe for Intermediate- and Advanced-Level Dancers: Solo	55									✓	✓		✓	✓
Recipe for Intermediate- and Advanced-Level Dancers: Ensemble	57								✓	✓	✓		✓	✓

Preface

I have a vivid memory of experiencing dance when I was four years old. I was watching the hydro wires and tree branches shift and sway back and forth while lying on my back looking out the window from the backseat of a moving car. It was during a long drive on a windy spring day. The branches were covered in tiny green buds and I liked the way they looked in comparison to the plain, straight hydro lines. The branches burst in and out of my field of vision, sometimes completely masking the swaying gray wires, other times looking like hands that were trying to pull the lines apart. I was fascinated by the explosion of images, the rhythm of the motion, and the contrasting textures of the wires and branches. I was mesmerized by the beauty and power of movement.

The world dances, and we can learn so much about ourselves and the world by studying the movement patterns around us. The creative movement exercises in *Perpetual Motion* identify many of these movement patterns and present them in ways that help students and teachers develop observation skills and creative movement abilities.

The exercises in *Perpetual Motion* can be adapted to complement any dance technique and can be applied to classroom use, dramatic arts, and physical education programs. I hope this collection of creative movement exercises will encourage dance teachers to let the outside world's spontaneous movement energy infiltrate their dance studios and their students' improvisational work, choreography, and performance dynamics. Conversely, I hope classroom teachers will let the exciting energy of dance into their daily studies. Their students will become physically active, will develop kinetic awareness, and will discover and explore their artistic and choreographic sensibilities.

The completion of *Perpetual Motion* marks my 25th anniversary of teaching dance and dramatic movement to young people, preprofessional and professional dancers, and actors. I can't think of a better way to celebrate than to share some of the knowledge I have gained while working with so many challenging and dynamic people. *Perpetual Motion* contains some of my favorite creative movement exercises and integrated arts projects. I hope these exercises inspire teachers and students to explore, experience, and celebrate the world through dance.

Acknowledgments

I would like to thank everyone who allowed me to take photographs of their work: Ms. Deborah Stevens' grade 6 class from William Burgess Public School, Ms. Heather Moffat's grade 12 dance class from Don Mills Collegiate, my students at Pegasus Children's Dance Centre (and artistic director Jane Davis Munro for creating such a wonderful place to dance), Ranjan Bobby, and Briar Munro. Thanks to Jessica McEwan for providing the excellent examples of student artwork for "Dance Into the Picture." To all those who participated in the integrated arts projects described in the book: the Toronto Urban Studies Centre, Danforth Collegiate & Technical Institute, Kew Beach Public School, St. Joseph's College, King George V Public School, the Art Gallery of Algoma, and the Arts Education Office of the Ontario Arts Council for funding many of those projects and my work on the original manuscript of this book. Special thanks to Bella Pomer for her great advice and to Judith Patterson Wright at Human Kinetics who said, "Yes, we want your book." Also thanks to Amy Stahl, illustrator Dick Flood, and all the Human Kinetics staff who have helped to make the text, photographs, and design come together so well. And to my partner, Barry Prophet, who shares my passion and commitment for the arts and education: thank you for always being there.

How to Use This Book

Everyone and everything on this planet moves—the earth and all that exists above, upon, and beneath it. Some things move faster than the human eye can register; others move so slowly that a lifetime passes before a shift occurs. This is the dance that all people share. In ancient times humans used dance as a way of connecting themselves with the world. Dances were created to interact with the environment: the living creatures with whom humans coexisted; nature's cycles of growth, death, and renewal; and the patterns of the stars that traveled across the evening sky. Our ancestors created dances to celebrate and heal and to express their feelings and ideas about the world in which they lived.

The modern choreographer harvests ideas and images from the living forces that surround us, and she synthesizes their forms, rhythms, and patterns into something of her own design. Like a physicist, the choreographer explores fundamental elements such as time, space, shape, and motion; she develops movement theories and aesthetics as abstract as quantum theory and as visceral as gravity.

Perpetual Motion explores the moving world: the movement patterns that have have been with us since the beginning of time, and the movement patterns that are unique to modern society. Some of these patterns are constant and anticipated (phases of the moon), whereas other patterns occur randomly, often without warning (a forest fire or the collapse of a bridge).

The purpose of this book is to help you develop your eye as a choreographer. You and your students will learn how to observe, identify, and experience movement patterns as you work through the exercises in *Perpetual Motion*. Once these movement patterns have become familiar, you will learn how to explore and manipulate them as a modern choreographer does. You and your students will learn how to take simple movement patterns and refine them, exaggerate them, exalt them, and transform them into dance.

How This Book Is Organized

Perpetual Motion has six chapters. The first five chapters contain creative movement exercises designed to engage students physically, creatively, and intellectually. These chapters should be approached pedagogically, though teachers need not use all of the exercises from each chapter before moving on to the next level. The final chapter outlines several exciting integrated arts projects that are applicable for students of mixed abilities. These projects may be replicated; but more important, these projects are there to inspire teachers looking for new ways to share dance with their students.

Chapter One: Rules

The exercises in this chapter introduce creative movement concepts and movement terminology. These exercises are simple and highly effective tools designed to help students develop focus and concentration skills, group dynamics, spatial awareness, and peripheral vision. Students work in large ensembles, more often than not without any planning time. Nonverbal communication and "as it happens" problem-solving skills are honed. Students can perform these exercises without any previous movement experience; yet, because the exercises are so dynamically exciting, they are favorites with experienced dancers as well.

Chapter Two: Recipes

This chapter offers students the opportunity to choreograph original work on their own and with others. A variety of choreographic structures suggest a limited number of required ingredients that students must include in their dances. How those ingredients are packaged and what movement elements connect the required ingredients to one another is up to the students. Solo choreographic opportunities encourage students to explore personal aesthetics and dramatic performance skills, while working in ensembles offers students the opportunity to develop leadership skills, positive group dynamics, and generosity of spirit.

Chapter Three: Props

People move objects every day. In this chapter we explore common props (chairs, boxes, and balls) and uncommon props (giant elastic webs and stretch fabric). Students discover a variety of ways to animate these objects so that the objects take on a life of their own. When students work together to manipulate large props, they develop group dynamics as well as problem-solving and critical-thinking skills. All of these exercises are theatrical and can be adapted easily for dramatic presentations.

Chapter Four: Poetry and Prose

We talk all the time, but how much time do we spend listening to what we say? This chapter lets us look at language in a new way. Students are encouraged to explore sound, onomatopoeic words, and bizarre phrases that have become part of our daily speech. These exercises promote listening skills, language development, and performance dynamics; and they provide students with the challenge of translating spoken text and conceptual information into dance.

Chapter Five: Objects and Images

The exercises in this chapter always begin with a group discussion about a specific object or image. Students share their ideas and collaborate in small groups to create physically and mentally challenging choreographic works. These choreographic exercises utilize all of the skills developed in the previous exercises. The focus is on exploring personal aesthetics and performance dynamics and translating visual images and personal impressions into movement. Choreography created while working in this chapter can be rehearsed to performance readiness and presented outside of class in a more formal setting.

Chapter Six: Dancescape Projects

The four sample projects in this chapter show how students from elementary and secondary schools can combine elements of academic research and personal journal entries with creative movement concepts to produce dances of substance. Through dancescape projects, students translate information they have studied in school or collected through observation assignments into choreography developed in ensemble fashion. Dancescape projects connect dance with the world, with other art forms, with technology, and with physical and emotional environments.

Special Features

Perpetual Motion contains several special features that are beneficial to teachers. One feature is the three-step teaching template that is used consistently throughout the book. The template provides teachers with a successful structure that they can use to plan their classes. Another feature throughout the book is the use of random factors. Random factors play a part in our daily lives, and they play a strong part in creative movement work as well. *Perpetual Motion* also contains a glossary of movement terms that provides teachers with a user-friendly vocabulary adaptable for working with students of all ages and movement backgrounds. The final special feature is the learning skills reference chart, which teachers can refer to at a glance to determine which exercises will best suit their students' needs.

Teaching Template

As I started writing this book I realized the need to replicate the actual teaching structure I use when I lead creative movement classes. This structure follows a simple three-stage format: explore, observe, and discuss. In *Perpetual Motion* students will experience this process two times with every exercise: once when learning the original exercise, then again when manipulating that exercise with the suggested random factor.

When I introduce an exercise I ask students to explore it together. Then they work in groups so that they can observe one another. After everyone has had the opportunity to perform and observe, I ask the class to discuss their internal and external observations. Internal observations are personal insights gained through performing an exercise; external observations are personal insights gained through watching others perform the exercise. Every exercise in this book contains a list of questions that teachers can use to stimulate class discussions for both the original exercise and the accompanying random factor variation.

Random Factors

We deal with movement structures and random factor elements every day of our lives. On a pleasant day, cars traveling on a highway move along quickly and efficiently. During a snowstorm, the opposite occurs. Cars crawl slowly down the center of the road. Some cars spin, some crash, some are abandoned. The snowstorm is the random factor. It completely transforms the highway (movement structure) and makes it difficult for the vehicles (dancers) to travel in the anticipated way.

Imagine creating a dance based on the daily variations that occur on a highway when one applies the most basic of random factors: the passage of time. The sun rises and sets; there are active hours and quiet hours as humans follow eating, working, and sleeping patterns. The highway is nearly empty at dawn. As the sun rises, the highway overflows. Eventually the sunshine shifts to twilight, and rush hour has disappeared into quiet night. Distances between vehicles (dancers) expand and contract. Rush hour (tight, synchronized ensemble work) fades into easy late-night and early-morning traveling (spacious duets and solos).

Teachers using this book will experience a sense of shifting ideas and images. They may open the book to the first exercise, read it, and then have their students perform it. They can then ask their students to perform it again while incorporating the suggested random factor variation. Every exercise in *Perpetual Motion* includes a random factor variation, which, when applied to the original exercise, will force students to modify their work in a variety of ways. At times it will seem quite unlike the original because students will need to shift and adapt certain elements of the exercise to accommodate the random factors. This encourages students to take ownership of the exercises, to create their own random factors, and to manipulate the exercises in ways that appeal to them. You and your students can work the same exercise repeatedly using random factors of your own creation, or you can use the 83 random factor variations that are listed in appendix A.

Glossary of Terms

Before jumping into these exercises, you may want to familiarize yourself with the movement glossary at the back of the book. Words listed in this glossary can be applied to all art forms, and dancers and nondancers alike find them very user friendly. Communication is intrinsic to the arts. It is imperative, then, that students and teachers share a vocabulary that enables them to express their ideas, emotions, and personal aesthetics clearly to one another.

Learning Skills Reference Chart

What do students learn when they study creative movement? Aside from the obvious skills such as physical coordination, strength, flexibility, and a general state of health and well-being, creative movement helps students develop skills in concentration, listening, language, internal rhythm, problem solving, spatial awareness, group dynamics, generosity of spirit, dynamic performance, leadership, and personal aesthetics. Students will also develop the ability to translate information from one medium to another. The learning skills reference chart is a quick and easy guide for teachers who want to introduce or reinforce specific skills to their students. A classroom teacher working with students who have difficulty staying focused can refer to the chart and select exercises that will directly influence students' classroom behavior.

I like to use exercises that reinforce spatial awareness and problem-solving skills with my students before they perform on stage. These exercises give students the confidence and skills they need to deal with on-stage errors. I often remind students that every live dance or theater presentation contains errors: lines missed, late and early cues, costume troubles, lighting woes—you name it. Humans naturally make mistakes. Working through our mistakes without freezing, blaming others, or feeling embarrassed is something we need to work at in order to learn. Learning these skills develops more than the ability to perform well on stage. These skills influence the way students feel about themselves and, consequently, how they relate to the world.

Appendixes

The appendixes contain additional information teachers may find useful.

Appendix A: Random Factor Variations

If you and your students run out of ideas for random factors, there are more for you to explore and to be inspired by. For easy reference, there are 36 extra random factors as well as all of the random factors applied to all of the exercises in the book.

Appendix B: Warm-Up Ideas

Teachers with little or no movement background will appreciate these warm-up suggestions. This warm-up includes simple stretch and strengthening exercises, ideas for balancing, and across-the-floor movement combinations.

Appendix C: Discography

I like to expose students to the vast wealth of musical styles and traditions that exist beyond the pop charts. As students' musical awareness grows, their personal aesthetics expand to include new ways of seeing, hearing, and experiencing the world. This discography is a small sample of the music my students and I have enjoyed working with over the years.

Appendix D: Assessment Strategy

These are ideas for teachers who need to assess students' creative movement work. The strategy outlined is applicable to a wide variety of assessment styles.

Appendix E: Stage Picture

This is for teachers unfamiliar with stage directions—what they are and how to use them. It includes a diagram and exercise ideas for introducing stage directions to students.

A Final Note to Educators

Participating in creative movement programming is a unique educational experience for you and your students. Below are comments from students and teachers I have had the pleasure to work with. They represent a wide range of voices from elementary (general, enriched, and special needs) and secondary schools.

- "This program gave all my students an opportunity to experience success and to express themselves freely without the limitations of conventional written language. . . . My educational assistant and I could be seen with tears of pride in our eyes, tears brought about by a few students who were really expressing themselves (joyfully!) for the first time!" —Grade 7 teacher

- "It was all a wonderful experience for me . . . the most enjoyable part had to be performing in front of all the people in our school. It was almost magic." —Grade 6 student

- "What I learned from Janice cannot be found in books or in the classroom. Dance is not just about making a good looking product, it is about expression . . . it is another way of communicating, almost another language. Thank goodness there is something like dance that can be understood by all people, no matter where we are in the world." —Grade 8 student

- "Never have I seen such excitement and enthusiasm generated amongst my students over a school-related activity. . . . Not only did this workshop do wonders for their actual dancing skills, but the rapid growth in self-confidence, cooperation, motivation, and shared dialogue which I witnessed was marvelous!" —Grade 11 drama teacher

chapter 1

Rules

The exercises in this chapter are great for students of all movement backgrounds and levels. They help students develop focus and concentration, group dynamics, spatial awareness, peripheral vision, and problem-solving skills. These skills are important for all creative and technical movement work. Students learn to focus inward and control their minds and bodies; they become aware of other people around them and develop skills for communicating and working with others nonverbally. These are not just important movement skills, they are important life skills that are easily taught and reinforced through participation in these playful yet challenging creative movement exercises.

The Concept Behind Rules

Society creates rules to enable large numbers of people to function as individuals within a defined structure. Pedestrians walk on the sidewalk. Motorists drive on the road. Both groups follow traffic signals: green for "go," red for "stop," and amber for "slow." Though everyone pays attention to the traffic signals, the individual travelers feel and think different things as they move to their different destinations. No rule demands that pedestrians walk with 12-inch strides or keep their hands at their sides. Some individuals may do so, but many don't. They jog, shuffle, or skip. They walk arm in arm or with their hands on their hips. Motorists, too, show differences. Some whistle while they drive, others listen to the radio. Some drivers are calm and take their time, while others scream and honk at the traffic. As long as all the pedestrians and motorists follow the traffic codes, their safety is preserved; however, the rules allow for a great deal of individuality.

Keep the following in mind when working with the exercises from this chapter.

- Each exercise has specific rules that create a successful movement structure.
- Moving through these structures challenges students physically and mentally.
- Students will find that they are free to explore their personal movement ideas as long as they stay within the boundaries of the rules and structure.
- When random factor variations are added to an exercise, the structure of the exercise may have to be modified because the random factor variations will influence the rules.
- Use the suggested format of explore (dance), observe (show dances), and discuss (appreciate dances). This simple format helps to create an environment where students feel safe—safe to physically commit themselves to the activity; to explore their dramatic movement potential; and to communicate their individual ideas, feelings, and personal aesthetics to others.

Application

Whenever I teach technically challenging modern dance classes, regardless of the level, I like to include a creative element at the end. To me it is as important as the warm-up stretches, balances, footwork, and across-the-floor combinations. It may be as simple as letting the students choose the leaps, jumps, or turns for the final combination, or, if I have given them a long and difficult movement phrase that has taken a substantial length of time to learn, I often finish with a structured improvisational exercise that helps the dancers cool down both physically and mentally. Back to Front, Wave Walk, Flocking, and Add Water and Stir (all from this chapter) are great for this purpose.

The exercises I use to cool down and relax experienced dancers are challenging for novice movers. Elementary school generalist teachers who are looking for ways to introduce their students to movement fundamentals, as well as secondary school dramatic arts teachers interested in teaching dramatic movement skills to their students, will find the exercises in this chapter an effective tool for developing movement awareness and nonverbal communication skills, and for introducing choreographic concepts in an enjoyable and highly accessible manner.

Familiarize yourself with the movement terms found in the glossary on page 169. These terms are used throughout the book. Introduce the movement terms to your students and encourage them to use the terms regularly so that they gain confidence expressing themselves with this new vocabulary. Each time students perform an exercise, allow time for a class discussion. Use the discussion section following each exercise and the random factor variation sections to get ideas for directing student comments and observations.

BACK TO FRONT

Ask students to arrange themselves in two or three straight lines (maximum 12 people per line), standing one behind the other, with the leader of each line facing toward the open area of the room. Everyone should be standing in neutral position (legs hip-width apart, feet and head facing front, spine straight, arms at sides).

Those standing at the back of each line are the first to move. At the call of "go," the last student in each line runs to the front of the line and freezes in a shape. It can be any shape (besides neutral) and at any level (high, medium, or low). Immediately after the first students have made their shapes, those that are now at the back of each line run to the front and make a contrasting shape (that is at a different level from the person they have just run in front of). This process continues, with those at the back running to the front, creating new shapes that vary in level, quality, direction, balance, and focus from the preceding shapes. The students hold their shapes until it is their turn to run to the front again. The exercise continues until the lines can't travel any farther. If you are working in a large gymnasium, students may have three or four turns before the lines reach the far side of the room.

If you are working with absolutely novice movers, explore the notion of "contrasting shapes" before doing the exercise. Ask students to suggest contrasting

qualities they might apply to a shape (rounded, straight, twisted, high, low, symmetrical, and so on). Or you can make a mid-level shape and ask your students to make a contrasting shape that is higher or lower than the shape you have assumed. Walk around the students while they are frozen in their shapes and identify specific qualities. This approach gives students a visual and verbal reference, and it is most effective with young children or students in an English as a second language program.

The exercise can be performed in a limited space with participants running and freezing only once, or it can be extended with the lines repeating the process a number of times before they stop. If you have a large number of students, create three or four lines and have students work along the circumference of the room. This works well when the lines are placed an equal distance apart, all facing the same direction. The lines stay close to the walls, traveling around the room until they have returned to their original starting place. This way students get several opportunities to run to the front and make a new shape. Remind students not to repeat their shapes but rather to explore new ones each time they run to the front. When first introducing this exercise have all your students perform it at the same time. Later, divide the class into two groups: the movers and the audience. Ask the movers to go into their line(s) and perform the exercise while the audience watches, then reassign the groups so that everyone in the class can experience both doing and observing. That was the initial exploration and observation; now introduce the discussion.

Discussion

To get the discussion going, ask students to describe the exercise externally (what they observed while watching others perform) and internally (how they felt and what they thought while doing the exercise). Encourage students to use movement terms that you used when teaching the exercise, such as the key words *balance, level, contrast,* and *shapes.*

Ask students how they felt when doing the exercise. If a student says she really liked doing the exercise, find out why. If she says, "Because it's fun," find out what she thought was fun about it. Some students find it difficult to articulate their observations, but with a little encouragement, even a shy class should make some of the following observations. (These are actual observations from an eighth-grade class with no previous movement experience.)

- "It's fast and slow. You have to hold your shape for what seems like forever and be absolutely still, then run as fast as you can to the front [to form a new shape again]."
- "You are working in a group, but you don't have to talk about what you're going to do; you just make it up."
- "Everyone gets to become individuals, because everyone's doing a different shape."
- "You can create whatever shape you want when you run to the front to freeze as long as you are in a different level from the person in front of you."
- "I can really challenge myself with my freezes."
- "I didn't plan my shapes. I just ran up to the front and did the opposite of what the person before me did."
- "I had a hard time coming up with ideas for freezes, so I copied other people's ideas."
- "Some of the shapes I went into were really hard to hold; my muscles were shaking."

Developing observation skills and encouraging students to articulate their observations are critical to the creative movement process. Help students develop these skills by asking the following questions:

- "Did you ever not know when it was your time to move? (If so, why? What happened?)"

- "Did you ever find yourself going into the same shape more than once?"
- "What was the shape you found most difficult to hold? How did you manage to hold it (change it, rearrange it, focus harder, use more or different muscles)?"

Random Factor Variation: Physically connect to another person

In this variation, each student who runs to the front and makes a shape must physically connect with the person they have just run in front of. Ask students to connect with different body parts each time they run to the front and make a new shape. This encourages participants to come up with challenging and unusual connections, such as shoulder to ankle, head to head, wrist to toe, elbow to nose, and heel to knee. The connections can be supportive; for example, placing a hand under the other person's lifted foot helps that person maintain his position. Some connections can be potentially dangerous, such as sitting on a person's back or shoulder. Remind participants that they must not "drop their weight" onto each other.

Always demonstrate how to safely "rest" on someone. Demonstrate this by "sitting" on a student's knee or shoulder: hold your position and just lightly touch your body part to hers. Similarly, remind students that they mustn't pull each other out of position. If someone has her leg lifted at hip height, don't run up, put your shoulder under it, and lift the leg higher. Ask students to suggest some potentially dangerous connections, and then ask other students to demonstrate appropriate ways of connecting those difficult shapes together. Then divide into lines and try Back to Front using the random factor variation.

Once everyone has had the opportunity to try Back to Front with the random factor variation, have them perform it for each other. Once again, divide into two groups—the performers and the observers. Before the groups present the exercise, ask students to look for connections that surprise or impress them while they are observing each other.

Discussion of the Random Factor Variation

After everyone has seen the exercise performed, ask students to describe their internal and external observations using movement terms like asymmetrical, symmetrical, sharp, curved, balance, levels, direction, focus, and so forth as they answer the following questions:

- Did you see any shapes or combination of shapes that surprised or impressed you? (Describe the shape[s] and explain what you liked about the shape[s].)
- Was it difficult finding unique ways of connecting yourself to another?
- Was it difficult maintaining your own shape when someone attached herself to you?
- How did the random factor variation change the overall look of the exercise?

Student observations may lead to new ideas for varying the exercise. Some classes like doing the Back to Front exercise so much you can use it as a regular warm-up, applying different random factor variations each week. When the class runs out of suggestions on how to vary the exercise, consult the list on pages 151-154 for more random factor variation ideas.

FIVE TIMES FIVE

In this exercise students work on their own and create five contrasting shapes they can perform quickly and hold for an unspecified length of time. (You can vary the number of shapes depending on students' age or ability; for example, three for young children, and seven for more mature dancers.)

If your students have performed Back to Front several times, they'll have a wealth of shapes in their personal movement vocabulary. Before assigning the task, review the following information.

- Cartwheels, kicks, and turns are not shapes; they are actions.
- Shapes like handstands, the splits, or other difficult positions are not advisable. Shapes that cannot be assumed very quickly or held for an indefinite length of time are not appropriate for this exercise.
- The shapes should show great variety. Explore the use of different levels, qualities, and directions when creating the shapes.
- If you do a shape to one side, you cannot repeat the same shape to the other side.
- Shapes can be abstract, dramatic (communicating emotions like fear, curiosity, or weariness), or action-based (illustrating activities like sweeping, goaltending, or throwing a ball).

Have students work on their own for three to four minutes, which should be enough time for each person to create and memorize their shapes. Remind them to assign a number to each of their shapes. Then ask students to find a spot in the room where they can work safely without interfering with anyone else and stand there in neutral position. Tell them that you will call out the numbers of one through five (though that number may vary based on students' age and ability), and they are to go into their corresponding shapes as quickly and quietly as possible.

Start slowly. Call out "one," wait six seconds, and make sure everyone is frozen in shape #1. Then call "two," again making sure students quickly and quietly change shapes and freeze. Continue in this fashion, up to "five." Immediately repeat the numbers, calling them out a little faster. Repeat again, going even faster. Don't finish the exercise yet. After "five," go backward, calling out "four," then "three," and so on. Try calling out numbers out of order: "Two," "four," "one," "five."

Now that everyone has tried it, have half the class watch while the others perform their shapes and you call out the numbers. Work slowly and simply going from one through five and freezing at five. Switch the groups, so that everyone has the opportunity to present their work.

Discussion

After everyone has viewed the work, see if the class can compile a list of the different qualities found in the shapes. Some of those qualities will be asymmetrical, symmetrical, twisted, straight, wide, tight, open, closed, balanced, and askew.

- Did students create shapes that were similar to each other?
- Were some shapes surprisingly unique?
- Did students find it easy to remember their shapes?
- What did they do if they forgot a shape?
- Was it difficult to move into and out of the shapes quickly?
- How did changing the tempo affect the exercise?

Random Factor Variation: *Make the frozen shapes move*

Ask everyone to "animate" their shapes. Instead of being static, the shapes take on life: they move up and down, spin, travel forward or backward, or sway from side to side. It is important that the shapes remain true to their form while they move.

Demonstrate by using shapes similar to those the students are working with. Make a shape, then ask students to come up with five ways to make the shape move without really changing it. For example, if you are standing on one foot with your arms reaching over your head, you can

- slowly bend your standing knee down and slowly straighten it to maintain a slow, steady pulse (you can lift your heel up and rise onto the ball of your foot for added height);

- wave your arms and upper torso from side to side;
- keep your torso still and work your arms in opposition;
- hop on your foot, moving forward, backward, or side to side; or
- curl your fingers in to make a fist and then out again (small movements are just as valuable as large ones).

The preceding demonstration was a high-level balance with straight spine and arms. Next, try a contrasting shape, something tight and low, perhaps lying on your back with your legs and feet over your head, toes lightly touching the floor, looking like you are midway through a somersault. You can make that shape move by

- completing the somersault and doing several more, going forward or backward;
- gently rocking on your spine, moving the shape back and forth like a cradle;
- "walking" your feet on the spot (directly behind your head) as if you were treading on the spot; or
- carefully "walking" your feet toward your right shoulder, then your left shoulder, so that your legs are moving slowly from side to side.

Give students three to four minutes to come up with ways of animating their shapes, then have them work their animated shapes to various types of music. Choose extremely slow, suspended music (Gregorian chants or Japanese Shakuhachi music works well). Then try working with sharp, fast, rhythmic percussion music (for example, African and Brazilian percussion or Indonesian gamelan). Divide into two groups, with each group presenting for the other using both types of music.

Discussion of the Random Factor Variation

- Ask each student to describe an animated shape they saw someone else perform that made an impression on them. Make sure they explain why it impressed them.
- As a group, discuss working with the different music.
- Was one tempo or rhythm more difficult to work with than the other?
- Was it more enjoyable to watch the work performed quickly or slowly?
- Did the music add to or detract from the presentation?

You may wish to try this exercise with a variety of musical textures, tones, and rhythms. Refer to the discography on page 163 for suggested world music and experimental compositions and composers.

WAVE WALK

Before you begin you might want to review neutral posture and neutral walk. Neutral position requires that

- the spine is tall and straight, arms long at the sides, legs hip width apart;
- the body's weight is distributed evenly, so that no hip is favored, no knee is bent;
- the entire body is aligned so that the shoulders are over the hips, hips over the knees, knees over the feet; and
- facial expression should be neutral as well.

To walk in neutral requires students to maintain neutral alignment and to take smooth, even strides at a moderate tempo.

If your students are not familiar with the concept of peripheral vision you can introduce them to it with this simple exercise.

- Ask everyone to look straight ahead and extend their arms out to their sides at shoulder height.
- Now have students wiggle their fingers.
- Students should be able to see their fingers moving without turning their heads or shifting their eyes.
- Peripheral vision is the ability to see things that are at either side of your body while focusing straight ahead.

Ask 8 to 12 participants to stand in neutral position in a straight line that runs down one side of the room, facing out toward the performance space. If the class is working on a stage, the line should go from upstage to downstage along stage left, facing toward center stage (refer to the stage picture on page 168 for better understanding of these stage directions). Those not performing the exercise should watch from the audience area. Those performing the exercise should be told to stand close together, side by side. Students in the line should be able to see the people on either side of them with their peripheral vision. At the same time, they should not be so close together that their shoulders are touching.

Instruct the group to do the following:

- Walk in neutral, back and forth across the stage area.
- Walk maintaining a straight line, making sure that no one is walking faster or slower than their neighbors.
- Refrain from looking from side to side or talking while walking.
- When the line gets to one end of the room, participants should turn around to walk back across the performance area.

The use of peripheral vision will allow students to maintain their spatial relationship. The audience should see only the most downstage student (the one closest to the front of the stage) as the entire group moves across the stage in a straight, unwavering line. If anyone walks too quickly or too slowly the audience will see an uneven line, detracting from the intended overall look of the exercise.

Give students this important reminder:

● Students walking in the line will know if they are walking too quickly if they cannot see anyone on either side of them while they walk.

● Students will know they are walking too slowly if they can see people in the line walking ahead of them.

Throughout this exercise the walking should be smooth and unhurried. It doesn't matter which foot leads, nor does it matter if everyone is stepping down at exactly the same time.

Wait until the group has developed confidence performing the first step just described before introducing the following:

● Individuals can choose to walk, maintaining the straight line, or they may stop at any point along the way and freeze their position.

● An individual who chooses to freeze may not move again until the line returns and passes him.

● As the line passes, the frozen person may rejoin the line and resume walking.

This element makes the exercise more difficult. It is no longer a simple task of watching your neighbor with your peripheral vision. The space between walkers will now shift continually; the strength of the unified straight line now becomes a contrast to the individuals who drop out to freeze.

The only time a person may not stop and freeze is if that person is the only one walking. The exercise will end if no one is walking, so let students know it is their responsibility to make sure at least one person is walking at all times.

After students have accomplished the stopping and walking, suggest that those who stop and freeze do so using shapes that explore various qualities, levels, directions, and balances. This magnifies the contrast between the unified, neutral walking and the individual shapes. Make sure everyone has a chance to perform and to observe the exercise before discussion.

Discussion

As mentioned in the previous discussion sections, it is important to get students to describe their external (what they observed while watching the exercise) and internal (how they felt while doing the exercise) observations.

- "Was it easy or difficult for you to maintain focus while walking in the straight line?"
- "Did anyone have to adjust their stride to fit into the group?"
- "How did it feel when the person beside you froze?"
- "How did it feel when you froze?"
- "Was it easy to return to the line in one seamless motion?"

- "Why is this exercise called the Wave Walk?"
- "How is the Wave Walk a variation of the exercise Back to Front?" (First identify the similarities: For example, both use lines as their foundation, both require participants to move and freeze, and both allow freedom of expression in the freezes. Then identify the differences: In Back to Front, only one person moves at a time and the movement is fast. Wave Walk never moves too quickly, and the exercise starts with everyone moving together.)

Random Factor Variation: *Overlap two ensembles*

Try having two lines work at the same time. Here is the simplest way to preset the two lines so that there is space for the lines to "pass through" each other.

Place 8 to 12 students in a straight line in the center of the room. Instead of them all facing the same direction, have the first person face left, the second face right, the third left, the fourth right, and so on until everyone is facing the opposite direction from the people on either side of them. Now you can begin the exercise.

Ask everyone to walk in the direction they are facing. When they do, the two lines will appear—one going to the right and the other going to the left. Instead of everyone being close to the people they are walking beside, there will be a body's space between them. They must use their peripheral vision to maintain a straight line with those that are walking in the same direction as well as leave space for the people from the other line to pass through. It's difficult, but they must not close that gap.

As in the original Wave Walk, always have participants walk the full length of the room a number of times before you add the freezes. Both lines should be straight, but because the lines may be walking at slightly different speeds, they may not necessarily pass through each other at center stage.

Once it's time for freezing, tell people not to worry about which line they join up with after they have frozen and want to return to the walking. Sometimes the lines stay relatively even; other times the numbers become very lopsided. It doesn't matter. Try this variation several times. It's fascinating how many ways the lines will change.

Discussion of the Random Factor Variation

- "Is it good or bad that the number of people in the lines keeps changing?"
- "Did you find yourself favoring certain levels or shapes when you froze?"
- "Did you find yourself favoring a direction to walk in when returning to the line?"
- "How does it feel having people watch you perform something you don't have much control of?"
- "Is the Wave Walk the first exercise you have done where the element of chance plays such an important role?"

TAG

In regular games of tag, one person tags or touches another, and the person who is tagged is It. Everyone runs away from It, trying to avoid being tagged. In this exercise no one can avoid being tagged. When students move, they don't just run; they travel throughout the room, changing levels, timing, and direction. It is their solo movement opportunity. Students get this opportunity when they become It. Limit the amount of time, or number of beats to the music, that each person gets to be It. Sixteen beats of moderately fast music is enough time for It to travel through the performance area in a variety of ways before tagging someone else. If solos are allowed to take much longer, it becomes quite difficult for those who are frozen to maintain their shapes for the entire exercise.

Start by asking students to find a spot on the floor at a minimum of one body's length from anyone else. Students then freeze in a shape that they can hold comfortably for an indefinite period of time. Remind participants that contrasts in shapes are always important. Ask them to look around the room and, if necessary, modify their own shape if it resembles that of another.

To start, put on the music (instrumental with a clear beat). Count the first four beats so everyone has the same sense of timing, then call out a name. That person becomes It. It runs, jumps, and rolls over, under, and around the frozen shapes without touching anyone for 15 beats. On the 16th beat It must tag someone who is frozen and pass on the movement. When It touches someone, It must freeze while the person who was touched becomes the new It and starts to move. Continue until everyone has had at least one turn as It.

If, after being It, everyone passed the movement on by tagging from an upright position with an outreached hand, all of the new frozen shapes would look less interesting than the shapes they started with. Encourage students to tag using different parts of their bodies. This is very similar to the connecting the shapes variation in Back to Front. Suggest several tag ideas, such as rolling up to a frozen shape and tagging with the back, stepping over a frozen shape and tagging with the foot, or leaning onto a frozen shape and tagging with the elbow. This will help ensure that the frozen shapes at the end of the exercise are as interesting as the ones at the beginning.

This exercise is best performed to various types of percussion and atmospheric music. If you have the benefit of an accompanist, ask for a change in quality, timing, or actual instrumentation every few minutes. Vocalization is great as well. If you are working with a large class, have half of the group do the Tag exercise while the other half watches and creates sonic atmospheres through rhythmic clapping, humming, stomping, and finger snapping. (Or read the introduction and first three exercises in chapter 4, "Poetry and Prose," for vocal warm-up ideas; see pages 83 through 93.) Make sure the movers respond to the sounds as they move around the frozen shapes. The frozen shapes can take on various qualities. If the sonic atmosphere is haunting, the shapes will take on an ominous quality. It can be frightened by the shapes, jump away from them, cautiously approach them, or skitter past them.

Discussion

This may be some students' first experience performing an improvised solo. Find out how individuals responded to having to move without being told how, where, or when. Remind them that the shapes they created in the previous exercises were solos as well. Every time they ran to the front in Back to Front or froze in Wave Walk, they were doing a solo. The animated shapes in Five Times Five were solos as well. The only difference is that in this exercise, students have no preparation time, and they are the only ones performing movement while the rest of the class is frozen.

Use of basic movement tools will help students develop a larger movement vocabulary without requiring more technical dance skill.

- "How many of you changed *levels* while you were traveling across the floor?"
- "How many changed *direction* while moving through the room?"
- "How many changed *timing* (fast, slow, moderate) during your 16-beat solo?"
- "How many changed the *attack* or *weight* of a step or action?"

To better understand attack and weight, you might want to try this activity with your class: Start with everyone walking in neutral on their own around the room. Then ask students to lean forward every time they step down. Do this for several seconds, then change the emphasis or weight again. Go back to neutral walking, then ask students to let their legs gently float up before they step down. Go back to neutral walking, then ask students to travel as if they were walking into a strong wind, through a muddy swamp, or while dragging a heavy sack. Stop and discuss the different weights and attacks used in these walks.

Another idea to discuss before performing this exercise again is the use of frozen shapes for inspiration during solos. Students have already learned to watch each other's shapes in the earlier exercises; now they can take that skill and use it in their movement work. Ask students to incorporate at least one of the following suggestions the next time they do their solos.

- Roll or slither under a shape.
- Jump, leap, or hop over a shape.
- Assume someone else's shape, and travel in that shape across the floor. (Similar to the random factor variation for Five Times Five.)

Random Factor Variation: *Incorporate neutral bodies into the exercise*

Have everyone find a starting spot where they create a shape for their starting position, as in the original exercise. When the music, sound effects, or spoken text starts, the instructor touches or calls out the name of the first It. That person starts to move, changing levels, directions, weights, and timing; rolling, leaping, and running; and interacting with the frozen shapes as discussed previously.

Once It tags a frozen shape her solo is over, but she does not go into an original frozen shape. Instead, she must freeze in neutral. Once in neutral, she cannot be tagged again. At first the neutral shapes are in the minority; slowly they become the majority. The exercise takes on a different quality near the end. The audience sees It moving in a dynamic fashion through a crowd of frozen neutral forms. Make sure everyone gets to perform and observe before discussing this variation.

Discussion of the Random Factor Variation

- How did changing the frozen dynamic shapes to frozen neutral shapes change the dramatic content of the exercise?
- Did all of the neutral bodies freeze facing the same direction?
- Was one direction (e.g., backs to the audience) more effective? If so, why?
- How did the last two or three students who were It feel while they moved throughout the neutral shapes?
- What did the last student who was It do when there was no one left to tag?

Many of my students have commented on the power of this variation. An overwhelming number have said that it's like growing up. First you're a kid and you get to play and have fun, but then your world changes and you have less time to play; everyone wants you to be serious, work hard, stop laughing, and grow up. By the end of the exercise everyone has "grown up"—no one is left to tag.

WALK ON THE WILD SIDE

This exercise uses neutral walks as the foundation for exploring movement dynamics. It is a continuation of the walking exercise introduced in the Tag discussion. As before, students walk throughout the room at the same time, but in contrast to the earlier version, individuals create different walks that they must memorize and eventually present.

Everyone starts in neutral position, facing whichever direction they wish. Ask students to begin walking in neutral throughout the room. While walking, students should be focusing inward, observing how the body balances and shifts from one foot to the other, the position of their spine, the length of their stride, and the rhythm of their walk. After a minute or two of neutral walking, ask students to change one thing about their walk. They can change the position of a body part (spine, arms, head, knees, feet, etc.); the level, speed, or direction of the walk; the weight or balance of a step; and so forth.

Make sure the change is something that can be repeated for an unlimited length of time (walking on the hands or doing gymnastic walkovers or back flips is not appropriate). Ask students to memorize their change and call it Walk #1.

Have students return to neutral walking for a minute. This is important for two reasons: It is a good way for students to release the muscles from the twists and stretches of their Walk #1, and it reconnects individuals to their natural center.

Now ask everyone to change their walk again by doing something very different from their Walk #1. Once again, the way they move should be something that can be performed for an indefinite length of time. This walking variation should be memorized and called Walk #2. Ask everyone to review Walk #1 and then to review Walk #2. Then return to neutral walking. Ask everyone to create a third way of moving and call it Walk #3.

Ask ensembles of four or five people to present their walks while the rest watch. Start them off walking in neutral, then talk them through their variations, calling out Walk #1, Walk #2, and Walk #3 sequentially, out of order, or both.

Some of the walks may look like dramatic character walks, whereas others may be more abstract walks that exaggerate body parts or movement qualities. Ask students to verbally describe one of the walks they saw without saying whose walk they are describing. When a student recognizes one of his walks being described, he should go into the performance area and perform it. Did the walk match the description? Let everyone try to describe a walk. If you have a large class, ask five people to perform their walks, then have five different people try to describe one of the walks they saw. Ask those who described a walk to perform theirs, and have another five try to describe them. Continue in this fashion until everyone has had an opportunity to present and to describe.

Discussion

- How often did the spoken description clearly describe the walk?
- Did students incorporate words from the movement glossary?
- Did students have a limited vocabulary of adjectives and adverbs that were useful in describing the movements in this exercise?
- Does being able to describe an action make an individual a better mover?

Random Factor Variation: *Try to do everything at once*

Give students 30 seconds to review their three walks. Then allow them two to three minutes to figure out Walk #4, which is a combination of Walks #1,# 2, and #3. It may not be possible for every single element of all three walks to be present at the same time.

You may want to demonstrate with the following example.

- Your Walk #1 is traveling backward slowly.
- Your Walk #2 moves forward with the head and torso hanging to the right.
- Your Walk #3 is jumping into the air and clapping your hands over your head.

By combining these walks you might end up with a Walk #4 that has you moving slowly backward with your head and torso hanging to the right for one or two steps; then suddenly jumping up and clapping; and then landing with your upper body and head hanging to the right, ready to repeat the slow backward walk again. The three walks just described can be combined in other ways as well; you might want to let your class explore other variations of your three walks before combining their own three walks.

Discussion of the Random Factor Variation

- "Would you have ever thought of combining so many elements in a short movement pattern?"
- "Compile a list of the number of dynamic elements in each student's Walk #4."
- "Whose Walk #4 had the most dynamic elements?"
- Ask students with complex Walk #4s to teach their walks to everyone.

- Could these walks, and other movement patterns like them, make the Tag exercise more challenging to perform and more exciting to watch?
- Revisit Tag, asking the students to use greater movement dynamics in their work.

The following comments are from students after they had explored Back to Front, Five Times Five, Wave Walk, Tag, and Walk on the Wild Side.

- "We did an exercise where we had to use our peripheral vision. It was really neat. It was something you had to concentrate and rely on. I liked when we got to start dropping out with a blunt or sharp shape. Sometimes we got to do water poses like fish or surfing. It was really fun." —Grade 5 student
- "It taught me that dance is a lot more fun than I realized and that I shouldn't be ashamed to dance in front of people." —Grade 6 student
- "I was challenged both mentally and physically. When we worked the wave walk without discussing or planning what we were going to do it [was a] great challenge to keep my mouth shut!" —Grade 9 student
- "I now feel that I can use every part of my body more effectively. It's not just your face and words that act, but every bone in your body, every vertebra in your spine." —Grade 10 student
- "I feel I was challenged this week by reaching into the farthest corners of my imagination and creating all sorts of shapes and movements." —Grade 10 student

MIRRORS

Just like the mirror games we play in kindergarten, this exercise uses the leader/follower format. Unlike many mirror games, no one is supposed to win by tricking the follower(s). The leader and follower work together, trying to create the illusion that they are working in perfect unison with each other.

Ask students to form two equal lines and stand face to face about two meters apart. The students in the lines should be spaced evenly so that each person has a partner in the opposite line. Ask partners to stagger the distance between themselves and those on either side of them. Instead of having two perfectly straight lines, you will now have what appear to be randomly placed bodies, all facing toward the center of the room. On closer inspection you should have a symmetrical pattern: one half of the room mirroring the other in relative distances to their neighbors.

Determine which side should lead first. Remind leaders that whatever they do, they must always perform it smoothly, clearly, and slowly enough so that their partners can follow in perfect unison. Also, those leading cannot cover their eyes or lower their heads. If a leader covers her eyes (or lowers her head) and her

partner covers his eyes or lowers his head, how will he know when to remove his hands from his eyes, or lift his head back up? The followers must be able to see their leaders at all times so that they are able to read every movement the leaders send them.

At first have everyone perform this exercise at the same time, sometimes allowing the leaders to explore their own ideas, sometimes calling out specific directions for the leaders, such as exploring level changes, working only the arms, or exaggerating the torso and hips. Then try this exercise with half of the class working while others watch. After two or three minutes, switch roles.

Discussion

For most of the class, this will not be their first mirroring experience. Here are some questions to ask if students gain no new insights after watching this exercise.

- "Did you prefer having specific directions called out, or did you like leading without any outside direction?"
- "Does it look more interesting when pairs are working the same isolation, or does it look better when all of the pairs are working in different ways?"
- "What is the purpose of doing this exercise?"

The following are some student responses to the final question.

- "When you're leading, it makes you slow down and think about your movements, what muscles you're using, where your focus is."
- "Until now we've been moving the way we want to; now we have to follow someone else, whether we like what they are doing or not."
- "It's relaxing, like meditation or tai chi."
- "You have to really watch what the leader is doing. You have to read their entire body from head to foot, so it develops your ability to read large and small movements clearly and quickly."

Random Factor Variation: *Change the spatial relationships in the exercise*

Everyone will still work with a partner (ask people to work with someone different this time), but they will not form two columns facing each other. Instead, have everyone move around the room (walking, running, rolling, etc.) independent of their partners.

At a predetermined signal from you, everyone freezes; then, without anyone uttering a sound, the mirroring begins. Finding one's partner without moving from the spot is the most difficult element of this variation. It is important that immediately after freezing everyone starts to move very slowly. Students turn around on the spot to get a visual scan, focus in on their partners, and follow or lead as they see fit. No one should show that they are obviously looking for their partner, nor should they move quickly or noisily to try to attract their partner's attention. Also, since predetermining who is the leader is not permitted, partners must work that out for themselves from their isolated locations without obvious looks, nods, or signals.

Partners may be at opposite ends of the room, but regardless of the space between them, they must find ways to work smooth, continual actions that can be read from a distance. Let students slowly mirror for several minutes, then signal everyone to move quickly through the room again, walking, running rolling, and the like. Signal the freeze and repeat the process of moving slowly, finding one's partner, and mirroring. Ask students to see if they can change who leads during one mirror interval without having to be told and without signaling to each other.

Discussion of the Random Factor Variation

- "Were you able to read your partner's movements from a distance?"
- "Identify movements that were successfully communicated from a distance."
- "Identify movements that were unsuccessfully communicated from a distance."
- "Were you able to change the lead without signaling?"
- "Did other people ever interfere with your ability to see your partner? If so, how did you solve the problem?"
- "Did having obstacles (other people) to work around affect the exercise in a positive way or a negative way?"

Just for fun, try a variation with no partners. As before, have everyone move through the room, stop at a signal, then slowly move. Instead of looking for a known partner, participants can follow whomever they wish. Six or seven people may end up following the same person. Once in a while an entire class ends up mirroring one person. This happens by "chain reaction"—when E follows D, who was following C, who was following B, who was following A. When this happens, see how long the entire class can maintain focus. Finish the exercise by asking students to identify who they were following. It's an interesting way to see if there were common viewing patterns, such as whether most people followed someone to their right, someone a body's length away, or the like.

FLOCKING

Flocking is a more complex form of mirroring. It works best with groups of four but can be very successful with groups of three. Have each foursome stand in a diamond shape about two meters from each other (groups of three work in a triangular shape). They should all face the same direction so that one of the participants has his back to all the others. Call that person North, the person to his right East, the person directly behind him South, and the one to his left West.

Because North cannot see anyone, he is the leader. North moves very slowly, changing levels, working various isolations and full body movements just as he did in the previous mirroring exercise. Everyone behind North follows, creating the illusion of planned unity. In 20 to 30 seconds, North very slowly turns to the right (or left), and because everyone is following North, everyone slowly turns in the same direction. Now there is a new leader because the group is facing a different direction. Remember, the person who sees no one in front of him is the leader. If North turned to face East, then East is the new leader.

It is important that the leaders focus straight ahead and keep the head upright. Those following must be able to keep their gaze on their leader at all times. When first learning this exercise, leaders should keep their focus absolutely straight ahead as opposed to working diagonally, which is more difficult to follow. Also, because leaders are working with their backs to the followers, leaders must avoid arm actions that take place in front of their torsos, as the followers will be unable to see these. Arm actions to the sides and behind the torso work very well.

Play very slow, nonrhythmic music when students are first learning this exercise. Many people find that the most difficult element in Flocking is slowing themselves down to properly "feed" their followers.

Note: Remember, if you are working with an uneven number of students you can have some flocks of three, creating triangles as opposed to diamonds, and some flocks of four.

Discussion

- "How is this exercise different from the mirroring work in the previous exercise?"
- "How is it the same?"
- "Was leading, without seeing those following, a comfortable feeling?"
- "When was peripheral vision most helpful?"
- "When you were leading, did you tend to stay on the spot, or did you slowly move your flock forward, backward, or side to side?"

Random Factor Variation: *Combine two exercises*

Here's a way you can combine Tag and Flocking. Ask students to work in groups of five. Four of the students go into regular flocking formation; the fifth stands off to one side. Begin the exercise with those in the flock working as before, slowly and in unison. Once they have started, the outsider can begin the Tag exercise.

The outsider can move any way she wishes—inside and around her group—until she touches one of those in the flock. She then exchanges places with that individual: the outsider becomes a member of the flock, and the one who was touched becomes the outsider.

The students must make seamless transitions between being the outsider and being a member of the flock. One way to keep the transitions smooth is to insist that the outsider never touch the person who is leading the flock.

One of the challenging aspects of this variation involves contrasting the outsider's movement vocabulary with that of the flock. Encourage the outsiders to choose speed, texture, shapes, and actions that differ as much as possible from those of their flock. This random factor variation can help students develop ideas for solos within an ensemble piece.

Discussion of the Random Factor Variation

Have groups watch each other and then discuss some of the following questions.

- "Was it difficult being in the flock while someone was moving so quickly nearby?"
- "How did being the outsider in this exercise differ from being It in the original Tag exercise?"
- "Did this combination of Flocking and Tag lend itself to expressing dramatic situations?"

Most students feel that the answer to the preceding question is yes. Situations they have mentioned include the following:

● Feeling left out (at school, with friends).

● Coming to Canada (or any new country) and trying to imitate new mannerisms and understand new culture so that you fit in.

● Trying to get your family to see you as who you are, but never getting heard.

Here are some journal excerpts from secondary school dance/drama students after they had explored Flocking.

● "My favorite activity was doing the 'improv' dance. This was like an artsy version of follow the leader. In a group of three or four there would be one leader who improvised and the others would copy them. The exercise wasn't a big sweaty workout, it was like a meditation and relaxing session . . . everything flowed so smoothly." —Grade 10 student

● "Flocking is a great exercise, as well as challenging. I think it helps us develop skills we need as actors, such as peripheral vision, so we can be aware and sensitive to all the other actors' movements with us on stage." —Grade 11 student

● "What was good about this activity was that not only does it look so well put together, it lets people choose their extent of leadership ability, by being leader for however long or short they wanted. . . . Things really started to cook when two groups would intertwine* and people had to keep track of who to follow. It looked like the dance had taken hours to prepare!" —Grade 11 student

*Refers to random factor variation Overlap Two Ensembles (see page 13). Try it with Flocking.

PING-PONG

Ping-Pong is a very fast-paced exercise. It uses the observation skills developed in the previous mirroring activities and the exaggerated movement dynamics of Walk on the Wild Side.

Have students stand in two lines at either side of the room, each line looking toward the center of the performance area. The area between the two lines is left open for individuals to travel through. As in the mirroring exercises, those who are initiating the movement are called leaders. The first leader starts in the empty central area. You can select someone to be the leader if no one volunteers.

The exercise begins when the first leader starts to move. His action can be a short, repetitive abstract movement pattern that is repeated over and over again or a dramatic character walk that remains consistent so that it is easy to follow. Whichever style of movement the leader chooses, he must stay true to his choice as he travels toward one of the lines. As the leader approaches, those standing in that line mirror or imitate the leader's movement pattern or dramatic character walk. They must try to capture all of the leader's qualities. The leader will repeat his movements as he moves up and down in front of the line until he sees someone who has truly captured the quality of movement, facial expression, attack, and rhythm of his actions. The leader then establishes strong eye contact with that person, moves directly in front of her, and then changes position with her (easily done if the leader and the follower rotate to the right), maintaining the movement pattern or character walk until the exchange is complete. The follower is now the leader, maintaining the action in front of the line; the former leader is now standing in the line in the follower's place. Everyone in that line can now rest, standing in neutral position. Those in the opposite line have been standing in neutral, watching the first line work. Now it is their turn.

The new leader now moves toward the other line. As the leader travels toward the center of the room, she transforms the original movement into something new. Those in the line the leader is approaching mirror this new movement pattern or dramatic character walk. You may have to remind students that the leader must always offer consistent information for the followers in the line to reproduce. Once someone in the line has captured all of the movement pattern or character walk's qualities, the leader will change places with that person. This new leader transforms the movement pattern yet again, and those in the first line get ready to work once more. Repeat this process for at least five minutes or until everyone has been a leader at least once.

Discussion

- "Which type of movement was most commonly used by the leaders—abstract movement pattern or dramatic character walk?"
- "Which movement was the most challenging to mirror?"
- "Why was one movement more challenging than the other(s)?"
- "How did it feel to have so many people copying your movement?"
- "When you were watching the opposite line work, what did you observe?"

Random Factor Variation: *Interact with another without touching*

Have two leaders start at the center at the same time. Without any planning, both leaders create and establish their movement patterns or character walks. Instead of letting them move off to share these movements with those in the lines, ask them to work with each other in the center space. The two may move under, over, and around each other. They may be attracted to each other or repelled by each other. They may interact however they wish as long as they never touch (or talk to) each other.

Allow 10 to 20 seconds for this improvised duet, then the leaders each move to a line and share their movement as in the original exercise. As before, new leaders move into the central area and transform the old movement patterns into something new. Unlike in the original, they may not move toward a line to share this new movement until they have interacted with each other. Sometimes that means one new leader must stay in the central area, repeating her movement pattern, while she waits for the other leader to come and interact with her. Let everyone be a leader at least once before finishing the exercise.

Discussion of the Random Factor Variation

- Was this the first time students performed an improvised duet?
- Were the duets more successful when the leaders had contrasting movements or when they had similar movements?
- Did the duets take on a conversational quality (one moves, the other responds)?
- What were the similarities and differences between this duet work and the random factor variation combining Flocking with Tag?

IS THE HAND FASTER THAN THE EYE?

This exercise explores a single isolation: the hand. To lead this exercise use a drum, metal clicker, or wood block and mallet. If you have none of these, you can say "change" every time you want to initiate a movement.

Have students find a spot on the floor away from anyone else, facing any direction. In this isolation exercise students may move only one hand (fingers, palm, or wrist, or any combination of the three) whenever they hear the beat (or the word "change"). They must complete the movement before there is silence. The sound of the drum, clicker, wood block, or voice should last no longer than a second, so the movement must be very small and be performed very quickly.

Demonstrate the difference between moving and stopping with the sound, and beginning the movement with the sound and continuing through silence. (The first is what you want students to work toward; the latter is what often happens when students are trying to do movements that are too large.) Remind students that contrast of shapes is important and that they should explore a wide variety of shapes (bend at the wrist, extend index finger, turn palm upward) as opposed to repeating the same movement and familiar shapes (e.g., opening and closing fingers) over and over again.

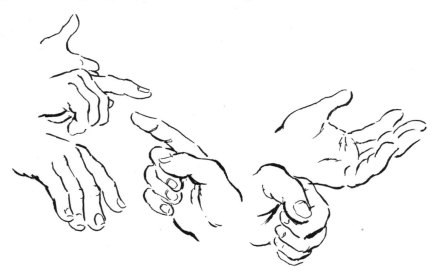

Begin the exercise slowly: Beat, then pause for four to six counts; beat, pause for another four to six counts. Participants will begin to anticipate the beats if a constant rhythm is maintained, so start to vary it once they have acquired the ability to control the shortness of their movements. Try beat, then one second of silence; beat, then two seconds of silence; beat, immediately followed by another beat, then four seconds of silence; beat, one second of silence; and so on. Make sure everyone stays frozen during the silences.

Discussion

- "Were you able to find a wide variety of ways to move your hands?"
- "Did you find yourselves repeating certain moves over and over?"

- "Which is harder—the very short, quick action, or the freeze between the actions?"
- "Try this exercise with different isolations, such as the face, leg, or torso, and then discuss ease and difficulty in these different areas."

Random Factor Variation: *Use movement vocabulary from an everyday activity*

Students apply the control developed in Is the Hand Faster Than the Eye? while performing an actual activity. In the original exercise the focus is on one part of the body. But in real life, we rarely do anything that way. When eating, for example, we use our fingers, hands, and arms to manipulate utensils and lift the food to the mouth. Once the food is in the mouth we use the tongue, jaw muscles, and teeth. This means the whole face moves, and when we swallow, the motion of the food traveling down the throat makes the neck move as well.

Ask everyone to imagine something they might have for lunch. It's important for students to have a clear image of the food in their minds. If someone is imagining soup, ask them what kind it is. If someone is imagining French fries, ask if the fries are crisp or soggy. Is the banana bruised, the peach juicy, the plum sour, the sandwich stale? It's vital that everyone has a very clear image of the food they are about to eat before they start.

The food must be "eaten" beat by beat. Remember, the beats are short (no more than a second long), and each movement must be completed in the space of a single beat.

The action of reaching for a spoon may take two, three, or even four beats. It might take one beat each to close the hand around the spoon, lift the spoon off the table, place the spoon in the soup bowl, lift the spoon, move the spoon toward the mouth, open the mouth, put the spoon into the mouth, pop the eyes open because the soup's so hot, swallow, gasp, reach for water, and so on.

Practice with everyone working at the same time. Then have students present their work four or five at a time. Ask those in the audience to watch carefully, observing the large and small details.

Discussion of the Random Factor Variation

- "Did those presenting chew beat by beat (bearing down the jaw or teeth on beat one, lifting them up on beat two)?"
- "Could you always tell what a person was eating?"
- "Did you know if the presenters liked or disliked their foods?"
- "Did the audience see specific information (sour milk, bone that caused choking, etc.)?"
- "Make a list of other activities you can try this with." (Washing the face and brushing the teeth or hair all work well.)

ISOLATION CONVERSATIONS

Try this exercise after you have done several single isolations described in the previous exercise. The structure of this exercise is the same, with beats (or voice) signaling the movement. There must always be stillness during the silence.

Have participants sit so that they are able to work one hand and the face. The hand and the face will not move at the same time. They will alternate. With the first beat students hear, they move the hand; on the second beat, they move the face; the third, the hand; the fourth, the face; and so on. Not only are the participants having to alternate between the two isolation areas, they are also trying to convey a dynamic relationship, or "conversation," between the hand and the face. The most difficult problem one encounters when first attempting this exercise is alternating the action. It can be a real challenge for some students not to move the face when they move the hand (and vice versa). To help students focus and isolate the appropriate action, you may want to call out "hand" or "face" when students are first learning the exercise. As time goes on participants should be able to perform this without an outside voice. If they get confused or flustered, tell them to stop, take a breath or two, and begin again. See how quickly people can work the hand-face relationship. After several minutes of everyone trying this exercise, have groups of four or five students perform it while the others watch.

Discussion

This exercise is great for getting people to animate their faces.

- How many areas of the face could be moved?
- Make a list of the areas of the face students mention and see how many ways they can animate those areas (e.g., eyebrows can move together, you can alternate their movement, you can arch or furrow them, nostrils can flare, cheeks can expand and contract).
- Western classical dance forms tend to ignore animated and highly stylized facial expression, whereas other dance forms demand it. Dance forms from many Indo-Pacific countries have very complex facial vocabularies. If you have students who have studied these forms, invite them to demonstrate and teach some of those movement techniques. Or you could present vid-

eos of these dance forms, available through libraries. If you are considering doing a section on mask and movement (as is common in many high school drama courses), this exercise and the random factor variation outlined next will be very useful.

Random Factor Variation: *Keep one part of your body frozen while the rest moves*

Have students use their facial muscles to create a "mask" for themselves. The mask can communicate an emotion (e.g., surprise, anger, confusion) or explore a quality (e.g., sunken, twisted, bloated). See if students can maintain that mask while they move in a variety of ways. Call out simple suggestions like "walk," "wiggle," "sway," "leap," or "hop," and let students explore those movements with their masks intact.

A great way for people to view each other's work is to have everyone stand in two straight lines at either side of the room, facing each other. Ask the person standing at the upstage end (i.e., the far end from the audience) of one of the lines to move in whatever manner he wishes (but always maintaining the mask) while he travels diagonally across the room to the downstage end (i.e., the front end near the audience) of the opposite line (see page 168 for a figure that illustrates stage directions). The next person to move is the one who is standing at the upstage end of the line that the first mover has just joined. She travels diagonally across the floor to join the downstage end of the opposite line. One at a time, students move diagonally across the floor to join a new line. Eventually the first two movers will be at the upstage ends of either line, ready to go again if desired.

Challenge students by saying that no movement or traveling pattern can be repeated by another person. For example, if someone has skipped across the floor, no one else may do the same style of skip. Someone may skip backward or swing her arms in a different way, but the movement must be obviously different from that of the first person who skipped.

Discussion of the Random Factor Variation

- How many people chose a movement pattern that complemented their mask?
- How many people chose a movement pattern that was in contrast to their mask?
- Were most of the combinations of mask and movement character-based?
- Were there any abstract mask and movement combinations?
- Was one approach more successful than the others?

Some of the mask and movement combinations can be quite funny. You may want to adapt this exercise for *commedia dell'arte,* mime, or clowning studies.

BODY PARTS

These combined isolations help students explore new movement vocabulary through limiting the use of specific body parts. Introduce this exercise by having everyone work with the same isolations. For example, ask students to explore different ways of moving across the floor while keeping the right elbow attached to the left foot. Remind them to keep trying new ways of moving: high, low, fast, slow, smooth, erratic, and so on. After they have worked the elbow–foot combination, have them try another, such as the forehead attached to the left biceps, or the inside thighs "glued" together.

Next, ask each participant to select his own isolation combination. Once students have made their selection, they should create a movement sequence that includes a minimum of three different ways of moving while maintaining that isolation.

If you feel your students need to try a sample sequence together, have them go back to the forehead attached to the left biceps isolation. Already students should have a good vocabulary for this isolation. See how well they are able to use that vocabulary in a movement sequence. Or you can demonstrate a sequence for that isolation. Start with a slow and heavy walk (with the head and left arm moving up and down in a sad, self-involved manner), reach the right arm up to the ceiling, tilt then balance on the right foot with the left leg extended in the air for just a moment. Lower the left leg and return to the upright stance. Then tilt and balance on the left foot with the right leg extended in the air. Lower the right leg, return to the upright stance, and repeat again, lifting the left leg and then the right, creating a pendulum or metronome-like motion. Then slowly sink to the floor and sit, rocking back and forth with the head tightly wrapped in the left arm.

Give students a maximum of five minutes to create their own isolations, create their movement sequences, and memorize the work. Have half the group watch while the other half performs their movement sequences.

Discussion

- Were there similarities in the isolation combinations chosen?
- Did students with similar isolations create contrasting movement sequences?
- Did many of the movement sequences communicate an emotion or a dramatic situation?
- Did the isolation add to or detract from the more dancerly movements (as in the suggested demonstration, did the tilts look more interesting because the forehead was connected to the left bicep)?
- List the most unusual isolation combinations presented and identify the reasons behind their uniqueness.

Random Factor Variation: *Emphasize contrasting movements*

Ask students to work with two or three other people whose isolation combinations contrast theirs. The contrasting isolations should employ different body parts; "big toe to knee" and "both elbows touching" are contrasting isolations. Without planning time, look at the work again. Invite one group to perform their movement sequences, first by starting from different corners and simply traveling across the room at the same time, then a second time with everyone starting in a huddled clump at center stage and moving out in different directions away from each other.

Ask the next group to present their sequences beginning just as the first group did, by starting from different corners and traveling across the room. Then ask them to present their sequences a second time, all starting from upstage left and traveling out—one moving straight across to upstage right, one diagonally to downstage right, one vertically toward downstage left. Ask a third group to present their patterns in the same way that the others began, and then with everyone performing their sequences with different timings (assign fast, moderate, and slow). Continue this format with the remaining groups, coming up with a different contrast for each group's second presentation. Ask students in the audience to suggest starting positions and direction and timing changes for the groups to try.

Discussion of the Random Factor Variation

- Were the movement sequence contrasts apparent when each group did its first presentation?
- Did the contrasts become more exaggerated the second time?
- What were the most successful contrasts imposed on the groups?
- Did any of the contrasts imposed on a group create a dialogue between movers?
- Did any of the contrasts imposed force participants to explore aspects of their movement patterns they had not previously imagined?

ADD WATER AND STIR

This is one of my favorite exercises. My modern dance classes love doing this as a mental cool-down after a technically challenging class.

Invite three to five students into the performance area. Ask those that are viewing to assign and teach the performers three ways of moving. For example, one of the observers gives them a simple gesture: a thumbs-up, wave of the hand, kick, or hip wiggle. Another observer suggests one way of traveling across the floor: log rolls, hopscotch, or nervous pacing. A third observer teaches them a four- to six-beat abstract movement phrase: jump, run, run, turn, and swing the arms.

Students are allowed to use only these actions (as well as standing still in neutral) in the exercise. Those performing the exercise will be able to mix the order in which the actions are performed; change the timing; excerpt one or two actions from a longer phrase; repeat the movements; and explore levels, directions, and attack of these actions as they work throughout the performance space.

Allow performers no more than a minute to practice the three ways of moving and decide on their starting position (e.g., all offstage at different corners, all standing at center stage).

In the beginning it's best to work in silence. Once performers are ready, signal that it's time to begin. The performers were given their movement vocabulary only moments before, so the audience gets to watch a totally unplanned movement improvisation. The performers must use their peripheral vision, listen to the action around them (that's why this exercise works best in silence), and be sensitive to the contrasts and complements they are creating with their ensemble members. While performing they may copy each other, follow each other, and have "conversations" with each other. Wonderful movement variations can occur when students manipulate the movement vocabulary through timing, weight and attack, stillness, motion, and changes in level and direction.

This exercise is great for developing spatial awareness. Knowing or sensing what other performers are doing is a vital element of movement improvisation. Sometimes these pieces end themselves with everyone exiting or freezing, but improvising an ending isn't the most important element of this exercise. If students are still moving after two minutes, call time. Don't leave ensembles out there for too long; if they haven't concluded after two minutes, ask them to stop. As participants become more confident you may let them go longer. Remember to assign new actions for each ensemble.

Discussion

- "Did you ever not know what to do when you were engaged in this exercise?"
- "How did you decide what to do and when to do it?"
- "What did you react to most often (another person, own idea, external rhythm)?"
- "Did the pieces looked planned or improvised?"

Random Factor Variation: *Ring a bell for freedom*

Introduce the use of a bell, whistle, or loud hand clap as a signal to performers that they can do whatever they wish until they hear that sound again.

Assign new movement vocabulary, then have the first ensemble begin to work the improvisation employing the same skills they did in the original exercise (but using new movement vocabulary). After 30 to 45 seconds, ring the bell (or blow the whistle or clap), and on that signal performers can break away from the prescribed vocabulary and move however they choose. It should be a short burst of freedom. Ten to 15 seconds later, ring the bell again, and performers must return to the original movement vocabulary. Ring the bell a second and possibly third time before the improvisation is over.

Discussion of the Random Factor Variation

- Did the random factor add a new level of risk to the exercise?
- Were students able to move from the set vocabulary to individual freedom in a single beat?
- Did the exercise appear chaotic when the individuals were free to do what they wanted?
- Could you use other sounds to signal other actions (e.g., on the cry of "Fire!" everyone runs to center stage and freezes for three beats)?

This is the last exercise in "Rules." Before you go on to the next chapters, you may want to revisit your favorite exercises from this chapter and try adding other random factor variations to them (see the random factor variation list on pages 151-154 for ideas).

I use variations of Back to Front, Wave Walk, Tag, Ping-Pong, and Add Water and Stir all the time. When dance students come in to evening class mentally or physically tired, I'll start the class off with 10 minutes of fun, fast-paced movement exercises. That normally gets everyone back on track and ready to work.

Once you have completed "Rules" you may do one of two things. If you are teaching students with a dance background, you may go to chapter 2, "Recipes," for more technically based movement exercises. If you are working with novice movers or dramatic arts students, you may want to leave "Recipes" for a later time and go to chapter 3, "Props." The exercises introduced in "Rules" are revisited in "Props" but have a new slant.

chapter 2

Recipes

*A*ll of the exercises in this chapter encourage students to explore personal aesthetics and performance dynamics. The ensemble recipes offer students the opportunity to develop leadership skills, positive group dynamics, and a generosity of spirit. By giving young people opportunities for creative expression, we are helping them learn to make choices (personal aesthetics), to express themselves (leadership skills), to listen to and appreciate others (positive group dynamics), to accept ideas other than their own (generosity of spirit), and to learn to commit themselves 100 percent to the completion and presentation of a piece of choreography (performance dynamics). These are important skills for artists and important skills for life.

The Concept Behind Recipes

The exercises in this chapter are similar to recipes for food in the following ways:

- They have specific ingredients (actions or movements).
- They require preparation time (creating or memorizing).
- They can be served (performed) when they are completed.

As with cooking, some recipes are quite simple and easy to prepare whereas others can be time-consuming and technically demanding. Included in this section are the following:

- Simple recipe exercises for novice through elementary levels. These recipes help reaffirm movement terms and techniques as well as encourage students to explore their personal aesthetics.
- Complex recipes to challenge advanced dancers. Choreographic requirements in these recipes include having students manipulate lyrical movement phrases with unlikely direction and level changes. Allow for lengthy creation and rehearsal time.
- A theatrically directed recipe that incorporates spoken text. This makes a great special project for high school modern dance and dramatic arts classes.

When introducing recipe exercises, encourage students to adjust the required ingredients (specific actions) to fit individual tastes. If, for example, the required ingredients are a roll, a jump, and wavy movements that travel across the floor, each student should select the roll, jump, and wavy pattern she feels best fits her technical ability and personal aesthetics. As with real recipes, quantity is at the discretion of the cook (creator). Students decide how many rolls or jumps they want to perform unless the recipe specifically demands a set number.

Always encourage students to do more than the required ingredients and to work hard at creating interesting transition moves between the assigned actions. After all, if we were to compare five different oatmeal cookie recipes, we would find that though all contained oatmeal (the required ingredient), some would have molasses, raisins, or walnuts. The decision to choose one over the other is a matter of taste (aesthetics), availability (technical ability), and cost (time restraints).

Application

When teaching young dancers (8 to 10 years old) attending formal dance classes at professional studios, I introduce simple solo recipes almost immediately. These simple exercises require very little from the young dancer, save the desire to dance. Recipes let participants create their own movements while reinforcing technical skills that have been introduced in class. Within five or six classes young dance students are creating and performing short solo works with confidence.

More advanced dance and drama students enjoy the independence recipes offer. Creating solos, duets, and small ensemble pieces lets students take control of the action. They don't have to worry about being technically perfect; they don't have to do a move or combination they don't like. Once the theme or structure is given (and you can let students create those once you have used the samples provided), all the decisions are theirs. Of course, when working in small ensembles, students must learn to compromise and to be gracious at it, too.

What works with young people in a dance studio does not necessarily work in a classroom. Movement education in elementary schools is for everyone, not just those who want to dance and perform. The desire to dance, the required ingredient I rely on with the young dancers I mentioned previously, is not necessarily present in the average school student. With classes up to grade 8, I give students a 20-minute warm-up, then work with exercises from chapter 1 ("Rules"). When I finish "Rules" (and that takes weeks of presentations and discussions), I often skip "Recipes" and go directly to the props exercises presented in chapter 3. Once students have gained a real sense of confidence and thoughtful understanding of movement, I introduce them to some of the simpler recipes.

Recipe Preparations

The following 11 recipe exercises have been divided into seven categories.

Recipes for Novice Dancers: Solos

Give students no more than 10 minutes for creation and rehearsal. Students should feel that these solos are fast, fun, and effective. Remind students to add their own ideas and ingredients once they have developed movement sequences for the required ingredients. In these solo recipes the required movements are described using images and textures as opposed to technical vocabulary (e.g., "leap over a puddle" vs. *"jeter"*, "create the letter 'C' with your spine" vs. "contract"). They could just as easily be described in more traditional dance terms, but when working with novice movers dance imagery is very helpful. Students often respond to the images so strongly that they are able to perform technical skills in their recipe solos that they cannot easily perform in their technique class. I've seen young dancers who cannot balance on the balls of their feet in their technique class perform the most incredible one-footed balances in *relever* while performing the tightrope walk in recipe 2. All of the solos for novice movers help students develop performance confidence and give them the opportunity to share their ideas with others.

RECIPE #1

Required ingredients include the following:

- Starting low on the floor and beginning to move with sharp, quick "fire" arms
- Traveling across the floor with heavy "earth" steps
- Melting back to the floor with "watery" torso

Discussion

- Was it easy or difficult to create different movements for fire, earth, and water?
- Which element was the most challenging, and why?
- Was it easy for the audience to see and feel the difference between fire, earth, and water?

Random Factor Variation: *Change the quality of the action*

Try the recipe again with the following changes.

- Start on the floor and begin to move with slow, growing "earth" arms.
- Travel across the floor with splashing "water" steps.
- Return to the floor with crackling, "fiery" torso.

Discussion of Random Factor Variation

- Was this recipe as successful as the first one?
- Were the combinations of body parts and elements as easy as in the first one?
- How did the dancers solve the crackling, "fiery" torso problem?
- Which was the most difficult of the required elements, and why?

RECIPE #2

Required ingredients include the following:

- Walking on a tightrope for 8 to 12 beats
- Juggling arms while changing levels
- Watching someone on a trapeze with your entire body
- Two different types of wild animal jumps or lunges—one to start the piece and the other to finish it

Discussion

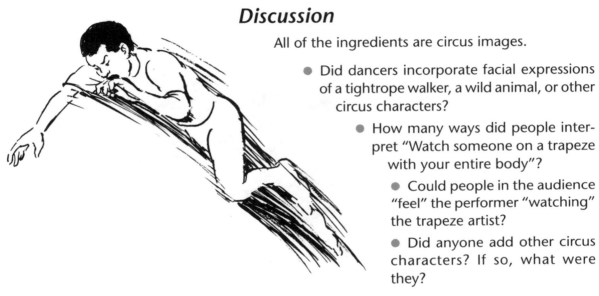

All of the ingredients are circus images.

- Did dancers incorporate facial expressions of a tightrope walker, a wild animal, or other circus characters?
- How many ways did people interpret "Watch someone on a trapeze with your entire body"?
- Could people in the audience "feel" the performer "watching" the trapeze artist?
- Did anyone add other circus characters? If so, what were they?

You may want to have students present these solos to circus music.

Random Factor Variation: *Have the audience watch from all sides*

Allow students three to five minutes to rework their dances so that there is no constant front. Then ask students to sit in a large circle, allowing for as much performance area as possible. Each person comes into the center of the circle and performs his solo with the changes he has made. Have the audience rearrange the circle often so people experience different vantage points.

Discussion of Random Factor Variation

European-based circus performers work in circular tents. The audience watches from all sides.

- "How many changes did each of you make to create a dance that could be seen from all sides?"
- "Did it feel different performing to an audience that was all around you?"
- "Did seeing some things from the side or back make them more interesting than when you viewed them from the front?"

RECIPE #3

Required ingredients include the following:

- Starting in an asymmetrical shape
- Taking 12 beats to change into a symmetrical shape
- Moving slowly downstage (toward the audience)
- Reaching out in different directions five times
- Jumping, catching or grabbing something, and freezing to finish the exercise.

Discussion

- Did the starting positions share many of the same qualities (e.g., low level, twisted arms)?
- What was the most common way of moving downstage?
- Identify the differences and similarities in the ways the arms and hands reached out.
- Were any compositions unique in their interpretation of the required ingredients?
- Identify what made the interpretations unique.

Random Factor Variation: *Change all aspects of the timing*

Have students explore this idea by reworking the piece using new timing requirements. You can either assign the new timing requirements or allow individuals to decide for themselves the number of reaches, the speed of traveling downstage, and the number of beats needed to move from their opening shape. Once students have reworked their solos, have them present their pieces again.

Discussion of Random Factor Variation

- How did the new requirements change the tension and quality of the pieces?
- Did the majority of students significantly change the action and quality of reaching?
- Ask students to compare their two versions and create titles for each of them.
- Ask students to identify three reasons for selecting those two titles.

Recipes for Novice Dancers: Ensembles

This exercise may be some students' first opportunity to work in a group and create a dance. Too much talking can become an obstacle to doing the work. Before students go into their ensembles, you might want to remind them of the following ensemble etiquette.

- Everyone in the group has something to contribute.
- Everyone should contribute at least one idea.
- Everyone supports other people's ideas by trying them out.
- Not everyone's ideas may get used in the piece. If your idea isn't used, that doesn't mean it's a bad idea; it just means that other ideas fit the piece a little better.
- Creative ensembles employ democratic principles.
- No one person is the leader; no one person can sit back and let the others do all the work.
- If people aren't willing to listen to each other and try each other's ideas, don't get into an argument; come talk to the teacher.

Novices often find it easier to create movement phrases to music, especially when working in ensembles. Music helps keep the ensemble members connected. Select a piece of instrumental music that has a steady, clear beat (no lyrics), and play it throughout the planning time and during the presentation. Allow 10 to 20 minutes of planning time.

RECIPE #4

Required ingredients include the following:

- Duet work
- Staying attached to each other while moving through three asymmetrical shapes with level contrasts
- Creating an eight-beat phrase that travels diagonally, and perform it in unison.
- Creating two contrasting eight-beat phrases and perform them at the same time.
- Finish in an attached symmetrical shape.

Students may have created their first movement phrases in Walk on the Wild Side when they combined walks 1, 2, and 3 to make walk 4. The only difference from the movement phrases students are creating now is that students must create them to fit special requirements (such as beats, direction, and levels).

When creating movement phrases in ensembles, remind students that they must be sure that everyone performing a unison phrase is comfortable with the vocabulary. Opportunities for individual abilities are available in solo recipes and many of the ensemble recipes when the required ingredient calls for "contrasting movement patterns." Someone who kicks and leaps very confidently may be teamed up with someone who does not. Their unison pattern should contain elements they both feel comfortable with (e.g., a roll, two side steps, windmill arms, and a slow melt to the floor) while their contrasting phrases will allow them to perform vocabulary that is in their own personal comfort zone.

Discussion

In this recipe dancers collaborate most of the time but still have opportunity for personal expression (the two contrasting eight-beat phrases). Learning how to compromise with another person's ideas and physical abilities and limitations is one of the most important elements in ensemble works. Ask students if they had to work through any of the following problems.

- "Did you and your partner have any differences of opinion about how to interpret the required ingredients?"
- "Did you and your partner have different strengths or physical abilities?"
- "Was it easy explaining your ideas for the piece to your partner?"
- "Did each member of the duet contribute equally to the creation of the piece?"

Random Factor Variation: *Change the number of participants*

Have each student perform her part in the duet as a solo. Allow only a few minutes for practicing; there should be no reworking of the original dance.

Discussion of Random Factor Variation

- "Did the solo pieces look complete as solos?"
- "Was it easier to perform the piece as a solo or as a duet?"
- "Did you see anything you would like to change in your dance now that you've watched your partner perform her half of the duet?"

You may want to give students time to work with their partners and make changes to their duets. If so, let them present their work again.

RECIPE #5

The required elements for the duet and the trio recipes are quite different. The duet demanded that participants be physically attached and that they create unison work that they both can perform. This trio recipe requires problem solving skills that focus on spatial awareness and level and direction changes. Required ingredients include the following:

- Trio work
- Creating a 16- to 24-beat movement pattern that everyone must perform
- One person working upstage (back area) only
- One person working downstage (front area) only
- One person working center stage (middle area) only
- Additional limitation: At no time can the people in the ensemble work at the same level or face the same direction.

Discussion

- What was the most challenging aspect of this recipe?
- Did students adapt a standing or high-level movement phrase for middle and low levels?
- How did each of the ensembles solve the problem of facing different directions?
- Did students use canon or round technique while performing the movement phrase?

Random Factor Variation: *Change the size of the performance area*

Ask ensembles to perform their pieces again but remove the upstage, center stage, and downstage limitations. Give groups 5 to 10 minutes to rehearse their pieces, with the dancers working as close to each other as possible. The level and direction limitations are still required ingredients.

Discussion of Random Factor Variation

- How did the reworked pieces resemble the original compositions?
- How did the pieces appear different?
- When might a choreographer want to use both variations?

Have the ensembles perform their pieces again, but add a fourth person to the piece. This person can move anywhere in the performance space using any movement vocabulary they choose. There is no need for planning or rehearsal. The fourth person can work improvisationally. After viewing, discuss the ways the fourth person's presence added dramatic tension. (Did it redirect the audience's focus? Unify the trio? If so, how?)

Recipes for Elementary- and Intermediate-Level Dancers: Solos

Solos normally require less creation time than ensembles. The required ingredients in these recipes are not too demanding. In 10 to 15 minutes students should have a completed piece. After seven minutes, stop and ask the students how things are going, then give them seven more minutes to finish up. These solo recipes encourage students to combine elements of technical ability, develop personal aesthetics as they interpret the required ingredients, and develop performance strength and dynamics. Musically, it's still easiest to play one piece of instrumental music throughout the rehearsal and performance time. A piece in 3/4 time (i.e., three beats to a measure) is required for recipe #6.

RECIPE #6

Required ingredients include the following:

- Solo work
- Music set in 3/4 time
- Starting and finishing the piece in a tight, knotted position on the floor
- A traveling pattern that uses triplets (a "down, up, up" step) as its foundation
- A freeze with the left leg suspended in the air
- A minimum of two jumps in any position

Remind dancers that each piece must start and end in a knotted position on the floor, but otherwise the order in which they perform the required ingredients and the number of transitional and original moves they create is completely up to them.

Discussion

- How many of the dancers created unique ways to move into and out of the opening and closing position?
- How many variations were there on the knotted position?
- How many variations were there on the left leg suspended in the air?
- How many variations were there on the jumps?

Random Factor Variation: *Emphasize a specific body part*

Have students rework their solos emphasizing one of the following:

- Elbows
- Knees

- Shoulders
- Hips
- Spine
- Neck
- Ankles
- Arm
- Hand

Discussion of Random Factor Variation

- Identify the changes made to the traveling patterns in each piece.
- Was the quality of the piece altered greatly?
- Did the movements appear to be more complex?
- Did this variation introduce students to body parts that had previously been ignored?
- Remind students that emphasizing specific areas of the body is a dynamic element that they can apply to all of their future choreographic work.

RECIPE #7

Required ingredients include the following:

- A footwork pattern that travels in a square (students may take up to 12 beats to complete the square) and is repeated at least once
- An angular arm pattern
- Circular torso movements
- A frozen shape that contains at least two triangles

Discussion

- "Were the geometric shapes always obvious to the audience?"
- "Had you ever thought of your body as being made up of geometrical shapes?"
- "Did you see other shapes besides the ones that were required?"
- "Which required ingredient had the greatest variety of interpretations?"
- "Which required ingredient had the least variety of interpretations?"

Random Factor Variation: *Add a hula hoop*

Give everyone 10 minutes to rework their solos, incorporating a hula hoop into their dances. Students may wish to use it in the traditional manner some of the time, but encourage them to find at least three other ways of manipulating the hula hoop. It can be tossed in the air or rolled on the ground; they can move through it, place it on the ground, jump around it, wear it over the shoulder, and so on.

Discussion of Random Factor Variation

- Did the hula hoop help to emphasize the idea of geometric shapes?
- Did the audience find themselves looking at the hula hoop more than the dancer?
- Did the hula hoop and dancer appear to have a relationship or conversation?
- How did using the hula hoop create additional movement vocabulary?
- Did the roundness of the hula hoop make the triangles in the frozen shape weaker or stronger?

Recipe for Elementary- and Intermediate-Level Dancers: Ensemble

The length of preparation time will greatly depend on the number of students in the class and the size of the studio, dance room, or gymnasium. Ensembles require not only longer creation time, but also more space to be created in. It's best to divide the working area into sections and assign each ensemble to a specific part. Ensembles may need to plan big, then work small for much of their creation time. If this is the case, allow each ensemble the opportunity to rehearse at least twice using the full performance area before formally presenting it to others. Other ensembles can use that time to work on specific details such as facial expression, eye focus, arm levels, hand styles, footwork, and angles of diagonal lines. Professional dancers work endlessly at this. It's called cleanup, and students at an elementary or intermediate level will benefit from this focused approach. They will develop a better eye for following movement, better communication skills for articulating the problems they see, and a better mind-body connection for blending their own movement styles with those of others.

RECIPE #8

Required ingredients include the following:

- An ensemble of three or more
- Creating a 16-beat phrase that is performed at least once in unison
- Within this phrase, at least one leap and one roll performed separately or together
- One person repeating this phrase two more times while the others work contrasting patterns
- A freeze during which everyone holds their positions for at least three beats
- Only one person onstage at the end of the piece

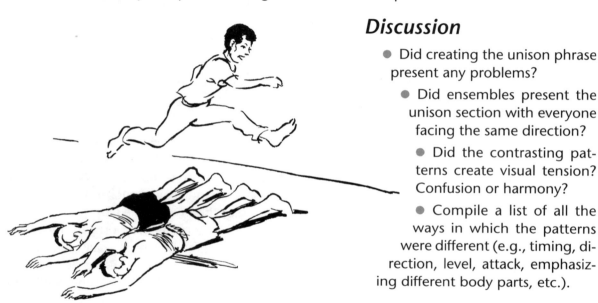

Discussion

- Did creating the unison phrase present any problems?
- Did ensembles present the unison section with everyone facing the same direction?
- Did the contrasting patterns create visual tension? Confusion or harmony?
- Compile a list of all the ways in which the patterns were different (e.g., timing, direction, level, attack, emphasizing different body parts, etc.).

Random Factor Variation: *Reverse the order*

Using the exact same vocabulary, ensembles must now start at the end of the piece (with one person onstage) and finish with the original beginning. Reversing the order does not mean that the dance must be performed backward, but that the sequencing of the piece is reversed. Therefore the middle section of the dance will still be the middle section, performed exactly as it was in the original version.

Discussion of Random Factor Variation

- Did the originally planned exits work well as entrances?
- Did the originally planned opening work well as a finish?
- It's interesting to see how often we create pieces that have weak or abrupt endings or beginnings. We don't always see it when we watch the piece in its original order, but it's very noticeable when we reverse the order.

Recipe Exploring Dramatic Potential of Movement and Voice

This recipe applies directly to dramatic arts or modern dance students who must learn to face the challenge of performing in choreography that requires vocal and dramatic skills. The technical level of dance used in this recipe is up to the individual ensembles.

The following exercise requires ensembles to select a word or short phrase that must be spoken and then interpreted through movement. Only one word or phrase may be used by an ensemble, but the interpretations of that word or phrase can have great variety. You can prepare students for this recipe as follows.

Ask everyone to work on their own to create a short (8 to 12 beat) movement phrase that interprets the phrase "It's so hot." Allow students to work for a few minutes, then ask everyone to present their phrases individually. Here are examples of some of the interpretations your students may come up with:

- Students may have interpreted the phrase to communicate hot summer weather and used exaggerated arm movements to wipe the forehead, rubbery or "melting" torso and legs, or created fan patterns with the hands, arms, or legs.

- Others may have interpreted the phrase to communicate food that's very spicy or a drink that's so hot it burns the mouth. Those movement phrases would contain lots of facial expression and upper body and gestural work.

- Some students may have interpreted "hot" as somebody or something that's really trendy or good looking. Did they watch the "hot" person or thing or become the "hot" person or thing?

- Others might have interpreted the phrase by showing someone stepping into a hot, steamy bathtub, shower, or sauna. These phrases may have contained lifted legs, extended feet, and pointed toes that carefully "tested the water," combined with fast actions of quickly hopping from foot to foot.

Seeing how one phrase can be interpreted a number of ways will help students with the required ingredients in the next recipe. If you and your students have never combined movement and voice you may want to explore some of the exercises in chapter 4 ("Poetry and Prose") before assigning this recipe. Sound Circle (page 86) and Five Times Five With Sound (page 89) are excellent exercises for introducing students to voice work.

RECIPE #9

Required ingredients include the following:

- An ensemble of four or more
- Each person entering at a different time and with a different movement pattern (of 12 to 24 beats)
- The common bond between performers: a word or short phrase that can be spoken by anyone at any time. Each person must perform a movement phrase immediately after speaking. This movement phrase must interpret the spoken word or phrase in some way, and at least once in the performance this word or phrase is spoken by everyone in unison.

Discussion

- "Was it easy choosing the word or phrase?"
- "Did the word or phrase inspire the rest of the creative work, or was it chosen after the movement was established?"
- "Could you hear everyone equally well when they spoke the word or phrase?"
- "Was this the first time you were asked to speak in a dance piece?"
- "If so, how did it make you feel?"

Random Factor Variation: *Work in total silence*

Students must now silently speak the word or phrase and work without any musical accompaniment. Ensembles may need to rework their pieces slightly so that they can get visual cues instead of sonic ones. Remind students that we still need to see their faces and mouths moving as they silently speak their word or phrase.

Discussion of Random Factor Variation

- "Was it difficult performing the piece without being able to speak?"
- "Were faces more or less animated in the original version?"
- "Did it matter that the audience couldn't hear the word or phrase?"
- "Did the silent phrase take on more or less significance than when it was spoken?"
- "How did the lack of musical accompaniment affect the piece?"

Recipe for Intermediate- and Advanced-Level Dancers: Solo

At this level, when asking students to create and perform their choreography, encourage them to choose their own music, as long as it is instrumental. This is an important element. Using instrumental music allows the dance to speak for itself and by itself. When choreographing to music with lyrics it's too tempting to just let the dance translate or echo the lyrics. This recipe requires out-of-class planning and rehearsal time if you allow students to create their choreographic compositions to music of their own choosing. All rehearsal during class time should take place in silence (so that no one's music interferes with anyone else's). The recipes for intermediate- and advanced-level students are opportunities for dancers to learn how to seamlessly blend their technical vocabulary with their theatricality and personal artistic vision.

RECIPE #10

Required ingredients include the following:

- Solo work
- A footwork sequence that explores turned-out, parallel, and turned-in feet using sharp staccato transitions
- A 20- to 30-beat movement phrase that incorporates two different types of jumps or leaps, a lunge, and a held attitude
- A segment in which the left foot remains "glued" to one spot
- Finishing by walking slowly upstage (away from the audience)

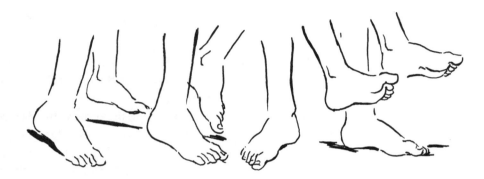

Discussion

- Explore the similarities and differences in the solos presented.
- How many walked upstage and finished the piece immediately after freeing their left foot?
- How many walked with their backs to the audience?
- How many faced the audience and walked backward?
- How many walked on a diagonal course?
- Have individuals discuss their decision-making process.
- Did students need to give themselves a dramatic character or quality to explore?
- Was the interpretation of the required elements purely abstract?

Random Factor Variation: *Change the ending*

Allow the pieces to stay the same except for the final required ingredient of walking slowly upstage. Students can now travel upstage in any fashion, using any timing they choose.

Discussion of Random Factor Variation

- Sometimes, changing something small can have a significant impact on a piece of choreography.

- How many used one of the other required ingredients to travel upstage?
- How many created an entirely new way of moving as they traveled upstage?
- How many changed the timing of the movement upstage?
- How did changing the final movement sequence affect each piece?

Recipe for Intermediate- and Advanced-Level Dancers: Ensemble

Out-of-class creation and rehearsal time may be necessary for this recipe as it may also take the students a good deal of time to rehearse the interlocking pattern that is one of the required ingredients. Encourage students to explore this required ingredient for all its technical and theatrical potential. This recipe demands strong performance dynamics and facial expression. The random factor variation is one that requires no rehearsal time. After all the work that goes into creating the piece, students enjoy being able to perform the random factor variation without having to rearrange their compositions in any way.

RECIPE #11

Required ingredients include the following:

- Ensemble work (three or more)
- The theme of hiding from oneself, from others, or from both
- Individuals select their own isolations (hand on face, knees locked together, etc.)
- Individuals create their own 16- to 24-beat solos
- While one performs her solo in real time, the others work fragments of theirs much faster or slower than real time
- Finishing with everyone "sharing" their isolation (e.g., one person places a hand on another's face, who in turn connects a knee to the dancer whose knees were locked, who in turn wraps an arm around the person who had her arms around her own waist, and so on)
- Creating and performing the piece without any musical accompaniment

Discussion

- How did having a theme affect the creative process?
- How did creating and performing in silence affect the piece?
- Did students create their own internal rhythms to complement their individual isolations?
- How did each ensemble decide the order for the solos and the timing relationships of the fragments that were worked in juxtaposition to the solos?

Random Factor Variation: *Explore environmental sounds*

Have ensembles perform their pieces while some of these environmental sounds are being played.

- Environmental soundscapes (of ocean, swamp, rainforest, crackling fire, etc.)
- Bird or animal calls
- Sound effects from old radio shows (e.g., doors opening, feet pounding, glass breaking)
- Sound effects from pinball or computer games
- *Machine Music* by Lou Reed (available on CD)

Discussion of Random Factor Variation

- How does the sonic accompaniment affect the movement work?
- Did it support the theme of hiding?
- Did the sonic accompaniment create an environment that overpowered the original theme?
- Did the dancers become part of the environment or appear separate and disconnected?

These 11 samples offer a few examples of recipe exercise work for novice to advanced dancers and dramatic arts students. Create your own recipe exercises for your classes by incorporating appropriate technical demands with variations in timing, level, texture, and emotion. Always plan your class so that there is adequate time for creation, rehearsal, presentation, and discussion. Use the list of random factor variations on pages 151-154 for more ideas.

chapter *3*

Props

*T*his chapter is all about manipulating objects and the fact that when you move an object, the object also moves you. Manipulating props develops focus and concentration, spatial awareness, and problem-solving and critical-thinking skills. Using large props that require a number of people moving together at the same time (or in different timing relationships) develops nonverbal communication skills and internal rhythm.

The Concept Behind Props

Every day we work with large and small inanimate objects. We move toothbrushes up and down to clean our teeth, carry bags and boxes of groceries, sort laundry, drive cars, rake leaves, shovel snow, and so on. In a single day we might perform many of these activities, and each "prop" we employ demands that we modify the shape, weight, timing, and motion of our bodies in order to work it properly. Though we move the objects, those objects are also moving us.

Application

Props are great for making simple movements look more powerful and intricate. Elementary school teachers who incorporate storytelling techniques into their language arts and drama classes will be able to integrate many of these movement ideas into their students' story theater presentations.

Secondary school drama teachers will enjoy the theatricality of these exercises. They show how people, without lighting or technical smokescreens, can be choreographed to create dynamic onstage environments.

Less-experienced dancers and those who are timid performers gain confidence working with props. They can hide behind the prop or work inside it. Sometimes these students become so involved in moving the props they are holding that they actually forget they are being watched.

Unlike the exercises in the previous chapters, the props exercises in this chapter have you introduce each of the objects through exercises that participants have already done. This process gives students the opportunity to explore the movement potential of each of the props as well as review skills that were introduced in chapters 1 and 2.

This chapter also contains a list of objects for you to explore. It is not an exhaustive list, but merely a beginning. Once you have explored the suggested props, try other objects and see how well they can be adapted to a movement exercise. Look around and determine what objects the people in your community come in contact with on a regular basis and what objects are rarely found. See if students react in one way to familiar objects and another way to those that are unfamiliar.

While working in this section, ask students to keep a movement journal and do the following:

- Take note of all of the objects they use in the course of a day.
- Focus on two contrasting objects (e.g., a safety pin and a bicycle) and describe how differently they make you move.
- Observe one person for 30 to 60 minutes and record how often that person changes his level, shape, balance, and timing because of the objects he has to carry or work with.

These journal entries will increase students' writing and observation skills and help them make connections between the everyday world and how dancers and choreographers take images and ideas from that world and turn them into a performing art.

CHAIRS

Our society spends a lot of time sitting. We slouch in chairs. We sleep in chairs. We eat, study, watch movies, listen to music, laugh, argue, knit, and read books in chairs. We are disappointed when we don't get to sit down on the bus during rush hour, and we show consideration for the elderly and infirm when we offer them our seats. We have chairs that provide comfort and chairs that don't. We have chairs that are used in specific professions, such as dentist and barber chairs. There are thrones for royalty, piano benches for pianists, canvas chairs for film directors, and swivel chairs for office workers.

Many modern dance companies have dance pieces that incorporate chairs. Chairs are very much a part of our environment; they influence our posture and movement patterns daily.

Try Back to Front (chapter 1, page 3) with chairs. The person at the back moves to the front holding a chair any way she chooses. When she gets to the front she freezes in a shape that incorporates the chair: standing on it, lying under it, twisted in it, straddling or sitting on it.

Try the same exercise again but don't carry the chairs; instead line up the chairs across the performance area and have one person at a time run up to a chair, assume a shape on or with the chair, and freeze.

Discussion

- "How did using the chairs influence the frozen shapes you made?"
- "How did the chairs affect the way you traveled to the front of the line?"
- "How did the presence of the chairs change the viewing experience?"
- "Was there a sense of humor, drama, character development, or story line?"
- "How did the exercise change when you no longer had to carry the chair when traveling to the front of the line?"

Random Factor Variation: *Communicate an emotion*

Compile a list of adjectives that describe human emotions. Sit in a circle and have each student contribute an adjective that describes a specific feeling. No one is allowed to repeat a word someone else has already used. After students mention the obvious emotions such as happy, sad, angry, tired, frightened, shy, and silly, encourage them to dig deeper so that they include words that describe less obvious but powerful emotions such as ashamed, anxious, blasé, confused, embarrassed, flippant, flirtatious, greedy, haughty, and so on.

Ask students to select one of the words without telling anyone else which one they have chosen. They must then find ways of communicating that emotion while sitting, circling, or somehow maintaining connection with a chair. Have students find a spot in the room where they can work on their own with a chair to create a movement sequence that they feel expresses the emotion they have selected. The movement sequence needn't be long—30 to 45 seconds maximum.

Allow students to work for three to five minutes, then ask everyone to return to the audience area. Place one to four chairs on the performance area and have students present their ideas. You can have up to four people present their work simultaneously; with any more than that, the audience will have difficulty following the individuals' work. Tell those presenting to start at the same time (some may wish to enter the performance area whereas others will want to start on their chair) and to freeze when they have finished. Most likely, the presenters will finish at different times. When a presenter freezes, she must stay focused within her emotion until everyone is finished. The audience's eyes will register the stillness and then refocus to where movement is continuing. Once everyone in the first group has frozen, ask the audience if they can identify the emotions that were being communicated. When a student's emotion has been correctly identified, that student may return to the audience area. Keep presenting the work in this fashion until everyone has had the opportunity to perform.

Discussion of Random Factor Variation

- Could everyone guess the emotions being communicated?
- What were the most common emotions? The most unusual?
- Were there any interesting relationships between those presenting (e.g., an angry, overbearing person beside a timid, frightened one)?
- Was there a group in which everyone communicated emotions that belonged in a specific setting (e.g., a waiting room at a hospital, a theater)?

BAMBOO POLES

Bamboo poles or thin wooden dowels that are four to five feet long are very adaptable, inexpensive props. If you are working with young children, you may wish to use shorter lengths and place plastic caps on the ends.

Return to the Flocking exercise in chapter 1, page 23. Have participants perform this exercise while each holds a bamboo pole. Encourage students to manipulate the pole by changing its level, direction, angle, and relationship to the body. Though they begin with the pole in their hands, they are not required to keep it there. They can place the pole on the floor or balance it on the shoulders. Students should explore the pole dramatically as well, transforming it into various objects: a magic wand, spear, fishing rod, telescope, paintbrush, and so on. As before, this exercise must be done very slowly. Ensemble members must move the poles in perfect unison to maintain the illusion that there is no leader, that everyone knows exactly what to do and when to do it. Maintaining adequate distance between flocks and individuals within each flock is important so that no one inadvertently hits a classmate.

Discussion

- "What difficulties did Flocking with the bamboo poles present?"
- "When you were leading, did you work all the levels with your body?"
- "Did you tend to remain vertical as you moved the bamboo pole to different levels?"
- "Did you physically change levels and shapes while manipulating the pole?"
- "Did the pole help you come up with movement ideas you might not have thought of on your own? If so, what were they?"

Random Factor Variation: *Create your own sounds*

Have students work in pairs to create a movement piece that explores the bamboo poles for their visual and sonic potential. Poles can tap the floor, be hit together to create beat patterns, rattled together, or rolled on the floor. Students can toss the poles in the air, jump over them, and transform them into specific objects. Give people time to create and memorize their work, and then have them present their pieces to each other. If your students have not worked through chapter 2, you should introduce them to "ensemble etiquette," outlined on page 43.

Discussion of Random Factor Variation

- "How did needing to create sounds shape the movement compositions?"
- "Did you purposely contrast the sounds with sections of silent movement?"
- "How did the bamboo poles influence the technical aspect of the pieces?"
- "Identify the various ways the bamboo poles influenced the emotional or dramatic content of the work."

ELASTICS

Purchase four or five 10-meter pieces of three- to five-centimeter-wide elastic (10-yard lengths of one- to two-inch-wide elastic). Hem the ends of each length, or coat both sides of each of the ends with glue or clear nail polish and let dry overnight. Either treatment lessens the chance of the elastic unraveling.

Have students work in as many groups as there are elastics; try to arrange an equal number of people in each group. Ask each group to form its own straight line, with approximately one meter (one yard) between students, and have everyone face front, hold onto the elastic with both hands, and stand in neutral position. Have each group establish their order: the person at one end is number one, the next person is number two, then number three, and so forth.

Use a drum, or clap, to call out beats. On the first beat the first person makes a shape and freezes (the elastic is still being held); on the second beat the second person makes a contrasting shape and freezes, then the third, the fourth, and so on. Start slowly. Beat (hold two, three, four), beat (hold two, three, four), and so on. After they have worked that tempo for several rounds, go faster: beat (hold two), beat (hold two). Then go even faster: beat, beat, beat. See how smoothly the groups can maintain the flow of movement from person to person, shape to shape, level to level. Students can move as far forward or backward as the elastic can stretch, adding new dimension to the contrasts. Participants must always maintain contact with the elastic, but they can hold or anchor themselves to the elastic with body parts other than their hands (e.g., elbow, foot, waist).

As students become more adventurous with the elastic, it is important to remind them that certain connections are potentially dangerous. **Do not allow**

- students to use the neck as a way of connecting with the elastic.
- students to wrap the elastic more than once around any part of the body (wrist, ankle, etc.).
- students to release the elastic quickly; this must be done slowly and carefully so that the elastic does not snap back.

Discussion

The Elastics exercise combines elements from several exercises in chapter 1.

- Can students identify the exercises that were used? (Back to Front, Tag, Is the Hand Faster Than the Eye?)
- What does the elastic add to the exercise?
- Does the elastic perform any service other than keeping the movers physically connected?
- Was it easier to hold difficult freezes when holding the elastic?

Random Factor Variation: *Move under, over, and around the exercise*

You may wish to try this variation in several ways, depending on the number of students and the size of the space you have to work in. Demonstrate the variation using one line of students in the following manner.

Have one group return to its elastic. Students line up as in the original exercise, with the person at one end being number one, the next person number two, and so on. Have a student from one of the other lines enter the performance area, standing in neutral position off to one side of the line. Establish a beat and ask everyone in the line to go into a shape one by one. Once everyone in the line has frozen in their shapes, invite the student who had been standing at the side to move through the shapes, going under, over, and around the elastic and the frozen bodies. When the student completes the journey from one end of the line to the other, allow those in the line to change their shapes, starting with number one, then two, and so on. When everyone in the line has changed level, shape, direction, and possibly body connection to the elastic, have another student move under, over, and around the elastic and shapes.

If you have enough space you can have all of the lines work at the same time in the following fashion: If there are eight students in each line, those students will make their shapes starting with number one and finishing with number eight. Then number one will carefully release the elastic and move up and back down the line, traveling under, over, and around the elastic and body shapes. Number one will return to the end and take hold of the elastic, and then it's number two's turn to travel up and down the line and then return to his spot. Continue this pattern until everyone has had a turn moving through the elastic.

Discussion of Random Factor Variation

- How did most people tend to travel as they moved up and down the line (fast, slow)?
- How often did people change their levels, tempos, or dramatic expression when moving along the line?
- Could the movers have interacted with the elastic in more dramatic ways? If so, how?

THE WEB

The web takes the elastic one step further. It requires preparation on your part but can be easily assembled, requiring more patience than skill.

Making the Web

To make the web you will need 22.5 meters (25 yards) of 3- to 5-centimeter- (1- to 2-inch-) wide elastic cut into the following lengths (see figure following these directions):

- For the center circle: 80 centimeters (32 inches)
- For the middle circle: 400 centimeters (160 inches/4 1/2 yards)
- For the outside circle: 560 centimeters (224 inches/6 1/4 yards)
- 8 "spokes": each spoke 150 centimeters (60 inches/5 feet)

Put the web together following these steps.

1. Pin the ends of the center circle together, laying it flat on the floor in a large open space.
2. Pin one end of each of the eight spokes to the center circle at equal intervals 10 centimeters (4 inches) apart.
3. Lay the spokes out flat and straight so that they radiate out from the center circle.
4. Measure each spoke from the center circle and mark 60 centimeters (24 inches).
5. Pin the middle circle to each of the spokes at the 60-centimeter (24-inch) mark.
6. Be sure to overlap and pin the ends of the middle circle to each other.
7. Measure each spoke from the middle circle and mark 60 centimeters (24 inches).
8. Pin the outside circle to each of the spokes at the 60-centimeter (24-inch) mark.
9. Be sure to overlap and pin the ends of the outside circle to each other.
10. There should be 30 centimeters (12 inches) of the spokes remaining for handholds.
11. **Before you sew,** check to make sure that all of the elastic is lying flat and is not twisted.
12. Firmly sew together the spots you have pinned.
13. After sewing, you may want to add glue to these spots for additional hold.

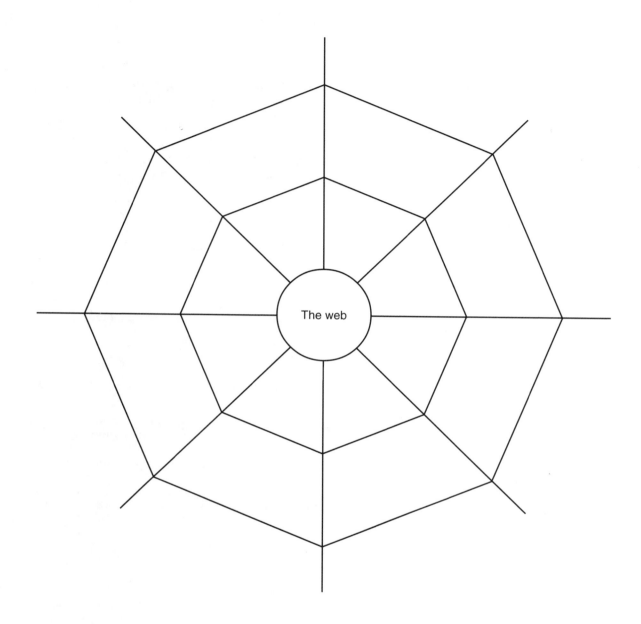

The web

Working the Web

Ask eight students to hold the web, with one person at each of the spoke ends. Remind them that the web will be moving and stretching, so it's important to have a firm hold on the web. Advise students to wrap the elastic spoke end twice around the hand to prevent the elastic from slipping or snapping out of their hands.

If all the students holding the web are standing and holding the web at the same level, the web will appear flat and will not read well from the audience's perspective. Ask students in the audience to suggest ways to make the web look more interesting. A simple way to give the web depth is to ask those holding it to alternate levels so that one is high, the next low, the next medium, and so on. Another way is to assign specific angles: those at the back (upstage) hold the web high, those holding the web at the center keep it at middle height, and those at the front (downstage) keep the web ends low. This gives the audience an excellent view of the web.

Have another group of students form a line to the right of the web. The first student in line moves through the web, working over, under, and around the elastic, just as was done in the previous exercise's random factor variation. Those students who will be traveling through the web enter to the right of the web, may spend some time exploring the central area, then exit on the opposite side. Unlike in the previous exercise, those holding the elastic web do not stay frozen. Instead, they can move, changing levels quickly or slowly, in order to make traveling through the web a challenging adventure. Once a person has traveled through the web, he can change places with one of the people holding a web end. That person can then go to the back of the line to the right of the web and wait until it is time to enter the web and travel through it.

Random Factor Variation: *Tell a story*

Divide into groups of at least nine (eight to work the web, one to travel through). Ask groups to create a short scene in which the person who is traveling through the web is an obvious character. Those on the outside can be in character or not. Those on the outside may speak, but only one line per person. The students traveling through the web may not speak but can react to the words as well as the actions of those on the outside. The person traveling through the web may also move around or outside the web. Allow students five minutes to discuss their ideas, and then give each group several minutes to practice on the web. Those groups not practicing on the web should continue to work on developing their story ideas or can try marking the piece without the web. Once everyone has had the opportunity to practice with the web, ask the ensembles to present their work to each other.

Discussion of Random Factor Variation

- How many ensembles created scenes with spiders and flies?

- What other characters and scenes did ensembles use?

- If all the ensembles worked with spider or fly concepts, try it again using the following: someone being interrogated, a child being scolded, someone having to make an important decision, running away from home, surfing the net. The web can be an actual web or it can symbolize feelings of being trapped or lost, making connections with others, or being manipulated by forces beyond one's control.

TUBE CLOTH "BODY BAGS"

Stretch fabrics are often sold in tube form, with edges found only at the beginning and end of the bolt. You can use this type of fabric to make "body bags" for individual, pair, and group work. Blends of cotton, polyester, and Lycra are the best for easy care and longevity. Make individual bags as long as needed to completely cover the person within. They should be adaptable to the range of ages and sizes you work with. It's simple for a short person to go into a large bag; the excess fabric settles to the floor near the feet. Unless you are working only with young students, allow at least two meters (approximately 6-1/2 feet) for each bag. Sew up one of the ends so that only one end of the fabric remains open.

Body bags for pairs or larger ensembles require more than double the length for individuals. Allow for a meter (approximately 3-1/2 feet) more than the sum of two body lengths. This body bag requires no sewing. Leave both ends open so that there are two ways to enter and exit.

If you can't find the tube form of this kind of material, you'll just need to do a little more sewing. Get cotton/polyester/Lycra fabric that is 140 to 150 centimeters (or 54 to 60 inches) wide and fold it so that the width of the body bag is 70 to 75 centimeters (or 27 to 30 inches) wide. Sew the two long sides together. Repeat, so there is a double row of stitching to prevent tearing. If you are making individual body bags, sew up one of the ends as well.

You need not make too many bags. Four to six individual bags and three to four larger bags for groups of two or three work perfectly for a class of 18 to 24. Students have as much fun watching as they do working in the bags.

Have four to six students go in the individual body bags while the others watch. Ask performers to stretch out as wide as they can, to reach up as high as they can, to press their hands toward the audience, and to pull the fabric tightly across their faces.

Have the students who are observing call out level and quality changes. Let everyone have a turn in the bags, switching over to the double body bags half-way through the process.

Return to Five Times Five from chapter 1, page 7. Working without the bags, have students create five shapes that they can move into and out of with ease and that they can maintain for an indefinite length of time. Allow students three minutes to create their shapes, then ask everyone to return to the performance area.

Have 8 to 12 students present their five shapes, then ask them to go into the body bags and perform their shapes again. Students can go into individual and double bags. As in the original Five Times Five exercise, you may call out the numbers of shapes or play music that has an obvious downbeat on which students change into their next shape. Have everyone present their shapes in and out of the bags.

Discussion

- Did the bags magnify certain movements or shapes and muffle or hide others?
- Was it easy to perform all of the shapes in the bags?
- Did the bag ever offer extra support for a shape?
- What shapes proved the most difficult in the bags?
- Were there any problems changing levels while in the bags?
- Did the bags change the emotional or dramatic quality of the work?

Random Factor Variation: *Work with only half the number of costumes or props*

In ensembles of four to six, explore movement inside and outside the body bags. Give each ensemble enough body bags for only half the participants so that the contrast between inside and outside is always present. Participants may want to have everyone do the same movement, whether inside or outside of the bags, or they may wish to explore a wider range of movement patterns and qualities.

Remind students of their introduction to the bags—how those watching called out instructions to those inside the bags. Directions for those inside the bags must be clearly stated and easy to follow. If students have not done much work creating original pieces in small ensembles, once again review ensemble etiquette:

- Everyone in the group has something to contribute.
- Everyone should contribute at least one idea.
- Everyone supports other people's ideas by trying them out.
- Not everyone's ideas may get used in the piece. If your idea isn't used, that doesn't mean it's a bad idea; it just means that other ideas fit the piece a little better.
- Creative ensembles employ democratic principles.

- No one person is leader; no one person can sit back and let the others do all the work.
- If people aren't willing to listen to each other and try each other's ideas, don't get into an argument; come talk to the teacher.

In addition, remind students that not everyone will be working in the bags. Only half the ensemble members will be inside a bag. If you feel that it is necessary, you can predetermine who works in the bags and who does not, though more often than not students can work this problem out without arguing.

Students who have explored some of the recipe exercises in chapter two or have participated in drama classes that incorporated ensemble work will need less time than those who have not. Allow ensembles to work for seven minutes, then check to see that all the ensembles have stopped planning and are actively rehearsing. Give the class another five to seven minutes for ensembles to finalize their pieces, then have each ensemble present their work.

Discussion of Random Factor Variation

- Did ensembles use the same or different movements for those inside the bags and those outside?
- Did those in the bags find it difficult to travel across the floor?
- Were certain timings more effective for those working inside the bags?
- Did ensembles explore contrasting timings of those inside and outside the bags?
- What other contrasts were explored?
- Did those working outside the bags react to the bags dramatically?
- Did the presence of the bags create an environment for the others to move through?

MORE FABRIC

Fabric has been used in performance work for centuries. Before the advent of stage lighting and special effects, one of the most effective ways to create a storm at sea was to use fabric. Lengths of silky fabric were spread across the performance area to create the illusion of water and worked from offstage by people at either end of each piece of cloth. The people holding the cloth created the water action by changing their armwork, level, and timing. Actors worked the narrow spaces that ran between the individual lengths of cloth. The fabric could start moving with only small ripples to communicate a placid body of water. Once performers entered the "water," the fabric manipulators would increase their arm movements. Soon the performers were caught in a storm. They could bend their knees and extend their torsos to create the illusion of swimming against powerful waves. The wave activity could increase as manipulators moved up and down, each pair alternating to create the undulating rhythm of crashing waves. The alternating also prevented the audience from seeing through the waves to the back of the stage.

Try variations of sea storms with your students. Buy enough lightweight silky fabric for three or four stage lengths. If you are on a tight budget, buy inexpensive polyester lining fabric. Be sure to hem the ends so the fabric doesn't tear or unravel. Assign people to positions at the ends of the fabric. See if, without planning, they can work the fabric from gentle ripples to wild sea storm, using the peripheral vision and mirroring skills developed in the exercises from chapter 1. Let everyone try manipulating the fabric; then try exploring the spaces between the fabric.

Wave Walk (chapter 1, page 10) can be easily adapted for this purpose. With four fabric lengths, you can have eight students working the fabric and five students doing the Wave Walk. Those doing the Wave Walk stand at one end of the fabric; one stands downstage (in front) of the first piece of fabric, the next stands between the first and second pieces of fabric, the next between the second and third pieces, another between the third and fourth pieces, and the fifth stands upstage of (behind) the fourth piece of fabric.

Remind those manipulating the water that they should keep the water at a level that does not interfere with the walkers' peripheral vision. Suggest to those walking that when they freeze they go into shapes that communicate images associated with water. It may take too long for everyone in your class to try both aspects of this exercise, but make sure that students experience one aspect before the discussion.

Discussion

- List the water-related shapes the wave walkers created. Were they water creatures, humans in the water, flotsam and jetsam, or aspects of the water itself?
- Was one of the preceding categories more successful than the others?
- Was it difficult for the wave walkers to work with the fabric?
- Was it difficult for those manipulating the fabric to work with the wave walkers?
- Could the audience see the wave walkers' shapes clearly through the fabric?
- Was it more effective when the fabric was low or high?

Random Factor Variation: *Explore a contrasting vocabulary*

If you have four fabric pieces, have participants work in four groups so that each group has a piece of cloth. Ask them to create a movement piece working the fabric in four different or contrasting ways and avoiding all water images.

Allow ensembles time to discuss, experiment with the fabric, rehearse, and set. Tell students to make their transitions between the four contrasting fabric or movement images as smooth as possible. The fabric work should be performed without any stops so that the contrasting movements flow into one another. For example, the fabric could start out tightly folded and enclosed in one student's arms. Another student in the ensemble slowly pulls one end of the fabric, others in the ensemble join, the tempo quickens as the fabric appears to be resisting them, but they finally manage to pull the fabric out to its full length. Once the entire length of fabric is completely exposed, ensemble members step away from each other and create a giant square by holding the fabric at waist height while standing in neutral position. The student holding the fabric ends starts to carefully roll herself, and then the others, into the fabric, creating a cocoon around the entire ensemble.

Discussion of Random Factor Variation

- Ask each ensemble to identify the four contrasts they employed.
- How did the ensembles come up with four different things to do with the fabric?
- Did ensembles select a theme or explore abstract patterns and relationships?

- How easy was it for ensembles to control changes in level, timing, and direction with the fabric?
- Was everyone in the ensemble a fabric manipulator, or did some ensembles have members who worked without touching the fabric?
- Were there many similarities between the ensembles? Identify the similarities and the unique ideas as well.

BOXES AND BALLS

All day long we use objects that are circular, cubic, or rectangular. Two of the simplest of these to work with are boxes and balls. Boxes of all different weights and sizes can be used in a variety of ways. Similar to chairs, they can be used in variations of Back to Front and Five Times Five. They can also be used in exploring levels (you can build with them) and as a unifier in Add Water and Stir.

Explore Add Water and Stir using boxes of various sizes. Have someone use a small jewelry box, someone else a box from shoes, boots, or a hat, and if possible find a large appliance box (from a refrigerator, oven, or the like) for the third person. Follow the directions for Add Water and Stir in chapter 1, page 34, and assign performers gestures and movement patterns that incorporate the boxes, such as pushing, opening, and hiding them. The size and the weight of the boxes will influence how the participants perform the actions and can produce some playful juxtapositions. If, for example, someone suggests a movement pattern that has students sitting on the floor trying to push their boxes with their right shoulders, the student with the jewelry box is going to look wonderfully silly.

Try Add Water and Stir using balls of various sizes and weights: large, light beach balls, solid basketballs, brightly colored juggling balls, tennis balls, and so on. Try the exercise a final time with four people performing the same actions, two using balls and two using boxes.

Discussion

- Was it difficult to come up with actions that were easily adaptable to both boxes and balls?
- Which types of actions worked best with which prop?
- Did the size and weight of the prop affect the movement to such a degree that the prop had to be abandoned?
- Does adding props change the original exercise of Add Water and Stir?

Random Factor Variation: *Become the object you are moving*

This is a really fun variation. Try to follow the ball's movement, and in a sense become a ball yourself.

Give each student a ball (or work in pairs if there isn't enough room). Let them get to know their props by throwing them, rolling them, and bouncing them against the wall or to their partners. They must always watch the ball as it travels. Spend several minutes at this, asking each student to focus solely on the ball, watching, listening, anticipating its every move. After three to five minutes, ask students to let the ball's movements move their own bodies (if it hasn't begun to already). As the ball bounces, the person throwing or catching the ball should allow his head, shoulders, torso, and knees to bounce or pulse along in sympathy. Once everyone in the class is allowing the ball to affect their movements, encourage participants to exaggerate their actions—to let their whole bodies become the objects they are moving. As the ball bounces high, the student following that ball jumps; as the ball hits the floor, so does its human counterpart. If the ball rolls slowly, the student slowly rolls along the ground. When the ball is thrown at a wall, the student does not have to run into the real wall; instead he can create an imaginary wall to run into and be repelled by. You may not have enough room for everyone to do this exercise at the same time. Have half the class watch as the other half works, then switch places.

Discussion of Random Factor Variation

- Identify the different ways students choose to translate the balls' movements.
- Did students feel connected to the ball while they followed its movements?
- Did they start to empathize with it?
- Did they get irritated with it?
- Did they try to slow it down so they didn't have to work so hard?
- Did the audience start to see the balls develop personalities or qualities?
- Can you try this exercise with any other prop?

MORE PROPS

Reread the introduction to this chapter and think of all the props people handle every day. The objects outlined in the following section are great to dance with. They can be used to create moods, environments, and dramatic characters.

Ladders

Ladders are great for exploring level changes and dynamics (how do simple hand isolations look when performed on ladders?). Don't limit yourself to keeping the ladders upright. Try placing five or six ladders down on the floor to create a star.

Brooms and Mops

Try using them to roll or push dancers on- and offstage.

Newspapers

Litter newspapers across the performance area and conceal dancers under some of the piles.

Fans

Use a variety of sizes. Dancers must develop movement phrases while keeping a part of the body concealed.

Eyeglasses

Develop characters, such as an absentminded person with a dozen glasses attached to clothing and body but never on the bridge of the nose. Try sunglasses and goggles.

Shoes

Have movers place contrasting shoes on their feet (slipper with construction boot, dress pump with sandal, cowboy boot with oxford, etc.) and create a walk that addresses both of the qualities or characters the footwear represents.

Claves (Rhythm Sticks)

Create hand dances using wooden claves or short wooden dowels.

Lots More Props

Can you and your students think of other relatively inexpensive items to use in a movement exercise? Start collecting. Go to thrift stores and garage sales, or ask neighborhood businesses to help out.

4

Poetry and Prose

D ance was humanity's first language. This chapter develops skills in language and listening as well as the opportunity to translate spoken or conceptual information into movement. Dramatic performance skills are greatly enhanced. The poetry and prose exercises remind us that we are always saying something when we move.

The Concept Behind Poetry and Prose

In this chapter students are asked to explore words—their meanings, rhythms, and lyrical qualities. Students learn to create and perform vocal scores to accompany their movement work. These vocal scores range from sonic atmospheres that work like soundtracks to absurdist theatrical dialogue that students can interpret in a variety of ways. Students are challenged by the blending of vocal and physical elements; the vocalizations become the impulse for all of the movement. They learn to listen not just to the surface meaning of a piece of text, but to the sound, rhythm, and multiple meanings of words and phrases. These skills then become the foundation for a number of the ensemble compositions. Silence, spoken text, "found sound," (sounds generated by striking, blowing, shaking, and rubbing objects not generally considered to be musical instruments—e.g., clapping rulers together, tapping a chopstick against the spokes of a bicycle wheel, rubbing the tops of wine glasses, and whirling lengths of vacuum hoses in the air) and dancer-generated sounds (clapping, stomping, finger snapping, and voice) are powerful sonic performance tools. Explore all of these elements, take a chance, and have some fun!

Application

If you teach high school theater or drama classes, these exercises are perfect for helping students get in touch with their voices and their breath. They are also excellent for introducing the notion of text and subtext (e.g., the character is saying one thing, but is that what he really means?). English as a second language teachers will find these exercises fun and accessible for their students with limited English. Learning a new language can be frustrating. Go outside, down to the gym, or to the drama room and give students an opportunity to laugh, move around, jump, and shout the new words they are learning.

Having read the preceding introduction, some dance teachers may be wondering how the exercises in this chapter apply to the training and technical development of their students. Obviously these exercises will be important to dramatic arts teachers, as they often combine movement and text, and those teaching English as a second language who need to find ways of incorporating vocabulary development into other areas of the curriculum, but how do they benefit serious dance students?

The poetry and prose exercises in this chapter are very important for preprofessional dance students because they introduce them to the skill of creating and communicating internal narratives. It is knowledge that will help them as professional performers. After all, what makes the difference between a soloist and a member of the ensemble? It is not necessarily that one's technique is better than the other's. More often than not, the difference between soloist and ensemble member is that the soloist injects intellectual and emotional dynamics into her movement that sets her apart from the others.

I am often employed as a performance coach. That means I coach dancers through challenging pieces of choreography. In its simplest format, this is the process I follow:

- I have dancers perform the piece of choreography I have been asked to coach them on.
- I discuss with the dancers their ideas about the piece—what the piece means as a whole and what each individual represents.

- Together we create a list of words and phrases that articulate the ideas and images contained in the dance.

- I then use exercises like those found in this chapter to help the dancers explore obvious and subtle ways of translating these words and phrases into movement.

- We then apply the emotional and intellectual awareness developed in working with the words and phrases to movement phrases from the actual choreography.

In this way dancers can stay in touch with their emotional and intellectual memories of those key words and phrases as we focus more and more on the original choreography.

Sometimes the most difficult aspect of this process is getting dancers to vocalize. You may find this true when introducing students to the poetry and prose exercises in this chapter.

Vocal warm-ups should became part of your daily class routine. If you are not familiar with vocal warm-ups, go back to chapter 1, "Rules," and have the class perform Back to Front (page 3). Ask students to make a sound when they make their shape. Each sound, like each shape, should contrast the previous shape and sound. If you have created any variations on Back to Front, impose vocalizations on them. For example, instead of running to the front you may have had students move forward in various ways: rolling, jumping, dragging a leg, and so on. Have the person at the front of the line create the sonics (e.g., clicking the tongue, humming, hissing) for the person moving forward. The person moving forward must adapt his movement to the sound. Once that person is in front, he takes over the role of being the sound generator and makes a new sound for the next person. Explore Ping-Pong, Walk on the Wild Side, and Tag in a similar fashion. Sound production can be the responsibility of the active or nonactive performers or those who are observing.

The poetry and prose exercises in this chapter contain a mixture of the lyrical and literal. They use words, phrases, and text and encourage sonic exploration. Best of all, these exercises are fun. Enjoy!

SOUND CIRCLE

Incorporate Sound Circle into your students' daily warm-up. It's a great exercise for the voice and the body. Sound Circle helps students develop internal rhythm, musicality, vocal confidence, and mental focus.

When introducing this exercise it is easiest if you act as the leader until students become comfortable initiating sounds. Please note that the focus is on sounds, not actual words. Onomatopoeic words like "boing" or "splat" are fine because first and foremost they are actual sounds. Other words, even simple ones like "yes" and "no," should not be used in the exercise. This will be true for many of the early exercises in this chapter. Avoiding actual words forces students to explore the textural qualities of their voices, just as the rules exercises in chapter 1 encouraged students to explore their physical movement dynamics without relying on specific technical dance skills, positions, or terminology.

Have students stand in a circle facing inward. The leader goes into a shape (one that can be comfortably held for a minute or two) and simultaneously vocalizes a short sound (no longer than two syllables), then freezes in the shape she has made. The person to the leader's right repeats the shape and sound, then freezes; then, one by one, each successive person in the circle does the same thing, producing a ripple or domino effect. After the person to the leader's left assumes the shape and sound, the leader creates a new shape and sound, and starting again with the person to the leader's right, the new action and sound travel around the circle.

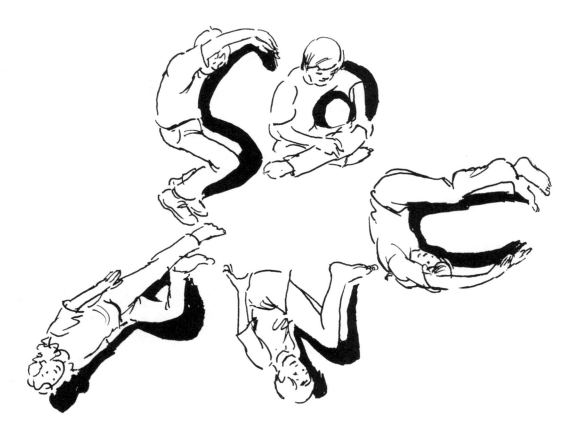

Encourage students to re-create the sounds as accurately as they do the shapes. You want them to imitate the different qualities of sound you lead them through just as they mirror the height of the leg, twist of the torso, or angle of the head you present them with in the different shapes you make. Be sure to work a variety of vocal textures: high, low, sharp, rounded, throaty, nasal, and so forth.

Have different students take over the role of leader. Depending on the size of your class, you can have everyone lead one action and sound, or ask the first six students standing to your right to lead two actions and sounds each. The following day ask another six, and continue until everyone in the class has had the opportunity to lead.

Discussion

- Were students able to reproduce the qualities of the sounds as easily as the qualities of the actions?
- Did the combinations of action and sound travel around the circle from student to student without pause?
- If there were pauses, identify the reasons they occurred (e.g., lack of focus, inability to hear the sound or see the action clearly, rhythm problems).
- How quickly can the actions and sounds travel through the circle?
- Do the actions and sounds tend to change speeds as they travel around the circle?
- If so, identify the reasons that this occurs (e.g., with certain actions and sounds, students' confidence level changes)

Random Factor Variation: *Turn the movement into a canon (round)*

Everyone has sung a simple canon or round. "Row, Row, Row Your Boat" and "Frère Jacques" are two popular ones we learn as children.

To turn Sound Circle into a canon, we first have to change the actions and sounds that freeze into actions and sounds that are continuous. For example, the action and sound of "hah!" as the left arm punches out and the right leg steps forward can be repeated on the spot with the addition of a beat of silence as the left arm and right leg return to neutral position. Try sending this repetitive action and sound around the circle. One by one, starting with the student to the leader's right, students join in until the entire circle is moving at the same time: "hah!," punch and step in to the center of the circle, silence, and step back.

When the last person, the student to the leader's left, has joined the "hah!," the leader sends a new action and sound that will travel around the circle, one student at a time. At the halfway point, 50 percent of the participants will still be performing the "hah!" sequence while the others are doing the new pattern. Use the silence from the "hah!" pattern for the sound in the new pattern so that the two fit together smoothly. The sound "whoosh" with the action of swinging the arms and upper body to the left is a good contrast to the "hah!" pattern. You can easily repeat this pattern over and over again by going "whoosh," swing to the right, "whoosh," swing to the left, like a pendulum swinging side to side.

Rhythmically, you want to freeze and be silent while the first pattern goes "hah!" and punches, then "whoosh" swing to the left, while the first pattern steps back in silence, and so on. Make sure that when students join the "whoosh" pattern they are going in the same direction. "Whoosh," those doing that pattern swing to the right. "Whoosh," those doing the pattern all swing to the left. Eventually the new "whoosh" action and sound overtakes the "hah!" sound and action. When the last person joins the "whoosh," the leader begins another action and sound pattern. Add clapping or foot stomping to create new action and sound patterns: clap, clap, "za" (jump forward on "za"), clap, clap, "zo" (jump back on "zo").

Discussion of Random Factor Variation

- Were students able to move from one pattern to another seamlessly?
- In choral work singers must listen to all the parts being sung, not just their own. Did students find it helpful listening to one action and sound while they were performing the other?
- Were students able to maintain one pattern while the person beside them was performing another?
- The person standing to the left of the leader has a difficult job. What is it, and what skills are required to perform it accurately?
- Was it difficult for the leaders to create new, contrasting action and sound patterns and introduce them at the appropriate time?

Once students feel confident working two contrasting patterns in canon, try adding a third pattern; once the class can manage three patterns, try a fourth. Discuss the difficulties.

FIVE TIMES FIVE WITH SOUND

Working with your class, make a list of 20 to 30 verbs that describe the way things move: for example, spiral, fall, skitter, glide, hop, drag, bump, splatter, undulate. Have each student find a spot in the room, and as a class explore ways of communicating a few of these words through movement. Don't work with music; instead, call out the words. Allow one minute for each word/movement relationship. Say each word a number of times and in a variety of ways as students work. Shout the word, whisper it, sing it, overenunciate it. Remind students to work the actions through different parts of their bodies as well as different levels, directions, weight of attack, and rhythms.

If you need to, review the exercise Five Times Five from chapter 1, page 7. The exercise focused on exploring contrasting shapes. Now that same exercise will combine contrasting actions and words. Ask students to work independently. First they must select five verbs that they will speak and physically animate at the same time. They should explore and practice their vocals while they physically explore and practice the actions. Encourage them to develop each of the words and actions so that the final product is much longer than five beats. For example, you might demonstrate the exercise using five contrasting verbs: swing, freeze, melt, bubble, and rise. Here's how those words might look and sound.

In a low voice, say "Swing, swing, swing, swing," while your body is bent and your head and arms swing as you slowly step forward. Next, shout "Freeze!" and try to step forward but find resistance. Shout "Freeze!" again, trying unsuccessfully again to move. In a soft, drawn-out voice, murmur "Mmmmelt" as your frozen torso relaxes and sinks toward the floor, and again, "Mmmelt" with your voice stretching the sound as your entire body melts to the floor. Overemphasize the first syllable of "BUB-ble" as your body, on the floor, reacts with a tiny lift of one arm. As you repeat "BUB-ble, BUB-ble," the other arm responds. As you continue "BUB-ble, BUB-ble, BUB-ble, BUB-ble," arms and legs react more energetically. Then you call out, loud and strong, "RISE!" as you extend your arms toward the ceiling. Again: "RISE!" (you sit up). Once more: "RISE!" (you stand, lifting arms, face, and chest toward the ceiling).

Introduce this exercise using the preceding example or with words and actions of your own. Allow students 5 to 10 minutes to create their own pieces, using words other than those you used in the demonstration. Insist that they explore and practice with their voices and their bodies. Have three or four individuals at a time perform—once in silence and once with students vocalizing their verbs.

Discussion

- How many students felt shy or embarrassed about vocalizing?
- Did working with specific verbs limit or increase students' movement vocabulary?
- Were there physical differences between the silent and the vocal presentations?

Random Factor Variation: *Create a dance map*

This variation requires paper and colored crayons or markers and for students to work in pairs. One person draws (using no more than three different colors) while the other moves. The idea is to draw shapes that interpret the actions performed by the mover. Those drawing can use circles, spirals, arrows, angles, or wavy lines—anything except writing out the verbs used as the foundation of the piece. The maps should be completed in the time it takes for the mover to perform her sequence three times. Switch roles so that everyone has the opportunity to create a map. Ask students to put their names on the backs of their maps so they can be identified later.

Now ask each pair to exchange maps with another pair. Let each pair look at the two maps they have received and then choose one to interpret through movement (they do not need to use spoken words in the new dance). Allow no more than five minutes for students to prepare their interpretations, and then ask them to present their work one pair at a time.

Discussion of Random Factor Variation

- Was it difficult to interpret the dance maps?
- Were any of the interpretations close to the original pieces?
- Were students able to identify elements or qualities of their original pieces in these new interpretations?
- Look at the maps.
- Did students have contrasting ways of illustrating similar actions?
- Do many of the maps look the same?
- Try interpreting the maps sonically, this time using vocalization instead of movements. You may wish to have a group of four students interpret a single map. Four voices have a greater range than two. Tell students that they can apply movement tools such as level, texture, order, timing, rhythm, and attack to the voice.

SOUNDTRACKS

Sit in a circle with your students. Ask everyone to think of the many different sounds (not using any actual words) the human voice can create. What are some of the sounds students thought of? Ideally your students included hisses, exploding consonants, nasal and throaty sounds, whistles, tongue clicks, and sighs, for these are the types of sounds you'll be exploring in this exercise.

To start Soundtracks, ask the student sitting to your right to make a sound and repeat it over and over. Once that sound has been established, ask the person sitting to that person's right to add a contrasting sound. Continue, with each successive person in the circle contributing a sound. When the fifth person adds a sound, it's time for the first person to stop. When the sixth person adds a sound, the second person stops, and so forth. Keep the sounds moving around the circle, never allowing more than four people to make sounds at a time.

Proceed around the circle several times. Encourage students to try new sounds. Impose a theme for each revolution around the circle, such as fire sounds, water sounds, city sounds, or rural sounds.

Discussion

- Find out how many ways your class can say "ah" and list them. Then connect the words in that list to words in your movement vocabulary. Your class my have come up with terms like high, low, ascending, and descending (levels); extended and contracted (timing and shape); soft and hard (weight of attack); and undulating, sharp, and repeated (rhythm and texture).

- Identify other similarities used in describing movement and sound.

- Ask students to demonstrate some of the ways they used changes in levels, timing, and rhythm in their sonic explorations in the circle.

Random Factor Variation: *Create your own recipe*

Ask students to suggest required ingredients for a solo recipe using images that can be translated into both movement and sound. You may wish to have them combine specific actions and dance imagery in their required ingredients.

Some specific actions that work well are the following:

- Sitting on the floor, rocking slowly back and forth in one spot
- Traveling from stage left to stage right in leaps or triplets
- Creating a circular pattern with the head and upper torso

The following dance imagery works well:

- Playing in dry leaves
- Walking on hot sand
- Bouncing like a ball

Explore these suggestions of specific actions and dance imagery with your class. Ask some students to create ways of slowly rocking back and forth while sitting on the floor. Then ask others to create rocking sounds that could accompany that action. The rocking can be interpreted in a variety of ways—a hummed lullaby or creaking chair. Ask some students to create circular patterns for the head and upper torso. Then ask other students to create circular sonic patterns that could accompany that—the droning buzz of a fly or singing "ahs" up and down the C major scale. Try the same thing with the image of walking on hot sand. Make sure everyone explores movement patterns and sonic patterns. If your class needs to continue to explore all of the suggestions, do so. Most classes need only a few examples to see how the relationship works.

The first step in the random factor variation is to create a recipe using images that can be translated through movement and sound. Students will create their recipes in silence, focusing on the movement as foundation for the vocal work to come. Students should need only 5 to 10 minutes to create their solos using three or four required ingredients.

Have one student present his movement piece in silence as the others watch. Ask that student to repeat his movement piece again while another student provides the soundtrack. Remember, no actual words should be used. Body-generated sounds like clapping or foot stomping are fine, but the focus is on vocal exploration. Continue presenting in this fashion: watching the movement pattern first in silence, then again with an accompanying soundtrack. Continue until everyone has performed their solo movement piece and created a solo soundtrack for someone else. Sometimes students creating the soundtracks will need assistance. You may need to suggest sounds for them; specific environments work well (depending, of course, on the solo it's accompanying). Sounds of cities, forests, and haunted houses, as well as emotional environments such as nervousness, confidence, despair, and innocence, are very effective.

Discussion of Random Factor Variation

- Did students hear sounds in their minds when they created their movement pieces?
- Did students in the audience hear sounds in their minds as they watched others perform their movement pieces in silence?
- Were any of the sounds students heard in their minds similar to those used in the accompanying soundtracks?
- Were students able to create effective soundtracks for the movers without any preparation time?
- What improvisational tools did vocalists use to create successful soundtracks or need to improve if the soundtracks were not successful?

WORD WORK

Instead of exploring vocalizations, this exercise encourages students to silently explore the shape of letters.

Create a list of words that describe emotions (or review the list compiled for the random factor variation of the Chairs exercise in chapter 3, page 64). Ask students to select one of these words; it should not have more than eight or nine letters.

Students now have to spell their words, using their entire bodies to create the individual letters (sign language is not appropriate for this exercise, because it is limited to the arm, hand, fingers, and face). They can spell the word with a combination of uppercase and lowercase letters. The letters should explore all levels—some can be created on the floor, some while standing, some at middle height. If a word contains double letters, as in "happy," each *p* should be different. Word Work is a variation of Five Times Five. The shapes now become letters, but otherwise all the other rules hold true. There must be level changes; students must memorize the order (spelling); shapes cannot be repeated; and during presentation, each shape (letter), must be assumed quickly and then held in stillness so that the audience can clearly see (read) it.

You may wish to explore a few letters with the entire class before students start working on their own. Try the letter *a*. Ask everyone to create that letter, and then see how many variations there are. Uppercase *a*s may be created with legs in a wide stance (second position) with an arm (from elbow to wrist) connecting the legs at the knees. This position also works sitting on the floor. You can create a lowercase *a* by sitting on the floor with the knees bent, the body and head curled in toward the thighs, and the elbows touching the knees, much like a sit-up. A class of 20 should come up with at least five variations on the letter *a*. If students still seem uncertain about the concept of using their bodies

to create letters, explore another letter. *S*, *R*, and *M* are good ones. Once students are ready to work on their own, allow them two to three minutes to create and memorize the letters that spell their words.

First, have two or three students at a time present their words. Ask them to hold each letter for three or four beats and then freeze in their final letter until everyone in their group has completed their word. Then ask each person in the performance group to present their word individually.

Discussion

Compare the different ways people interpreted the same letters.

- Which letter had the most variations?
- Which letter had the least number of variations?
- Did everyone utilize level changes so that their letters were not, for example, all flat on the floor?
- Were some letters difficult to read?
- Were some letters confused with others (capital I and lowercase l)?

Allow students time, if necessary, to fix any problems they had with level changes or clarity. Then move on to the random factor variation.

Random Factor Variation: *Combine two random factor variations*

Combine the random factor variations from Five Times Five in chapter 1 and Chairs in chapter 3. These variations were to make frozen shapes move and communicate an emotion.

Students must now inject movement and emotion into the letters they just presented. The emotion they must communicate is the one communicated by the word they spelled. The specific actions they impose on the letters may change as they move from letter to letter (just as they did in Five Times Five in chapter 1), but the emotion must stay the same. For example, someone spelling the word "nervous" might move in an extremely agitated way when spelling out the letters. He could shake, jump, look around, bite his nails, and pace. Because some of the letters are more conducive than others to shaking or jumping, students must make choices. Pacing probably works best with the letter *R*, which allows the freedom of both legs and feet, as opposed to the letter *E*, which has no "legs" to stand on. Someone presenting the word "sleepy" would probably work very slowly, perhaps yawning, rubbing the eyes, resting, and nodding off with each letter. Remind participants that they must use their faces as well as their bodies to communicate their emotions. Present in the same fashion as before.

Discussion of Random Factor Variation

- Were the original letters still identifiable?
- Were some of the letters more difficult to animate than others?
- Was the emotional content of the word clearly communicated?
- Did the movement between letters become as important as the letters themselves?

- Were there students who presented the same or similar words (e.g., tired or sleepy) but found very different ways to interpret them?
- Did everyone use facial expression as well as explore the weight, tension, balance, and rhythm in their bodies?

Have students present their work one more time with vocal accompaniment. Ask three or four students to create a soundtrack for one person's movement work. The soundtrack for "sleepy" might be filled with yawns, sighs, the ticking of a clock, soft humming, lulling sounds, snores, and the like. Those creating the soundtrack watch and respond to the actions the dancer performs.

- How did the addition of the soundtrack impact the movement piece, the performer, and the audience?
- Did those creating the soundtracks use multi-layering techniques (contrasting sounds at the same time)?
- Was there a soundtrack or vocal styling that really captured the feeling of the word being expressed? If so, identify the soundtrack's outstanding elements.

ONOMATOPOEIA

Onomatopoeia refers to words that are named for the sound associated with them. "Splash," "sizzle," "murmur," "hiss," "gong," "ping," and "whoosh" are good examples of these types of words. Sit in a circle with your class and create a list of at least 20 onomatopoeic words that students can use for this exercise.

Have students select one of those onomatopoeic words and then, working on their own, create three different movements to go with their single word selection. The actions or movement patterns should illustrate the word itself, not someone or something doing an action that produces the sound. For example, someone who selected the word "splash" should not move as if kicking or splashing water, but rather should become the splashing liquid itself.

Remind students to vocalize while they are creating their movements. Changing the vocal texture or timing of the word may inspire their movements. A splash can be short and fast or elongated; it can travel up, out, or down. Connect the voice to the action so that each of the three splashes has a distinct sonic accompaniment.

Ask students to perform their three sound actions as solos, then divide participants into small groups made up of similar sounds to present them a second time, and then into groups with contrasting sounds to present them a third time. Remind students that even when performing with others, individuals must always vocalize their words when presenting their actions.

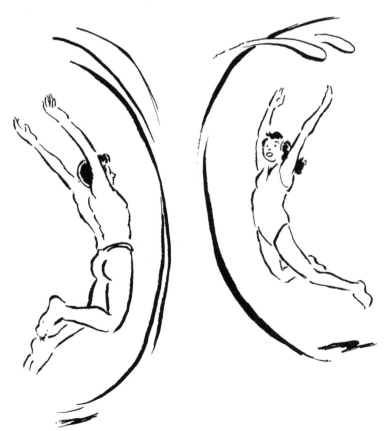

Discussion

- "Were certain words used by more than two or three people?"
- "Were those words translated in a similar fashion by those who used them?"
- "Did any of the sound–action relationships surprise you?"
- "Did any of the sounds and actions inspire you to think of new sounds and actions (for your own word or for someone else's)?"
- "Did any of the presentations have cartoon or comic book qualities?"

Random Factor Variation: *Combine three contrasting sounds*

Ask students to go into ensembles of three or four, making sure that they work with those whose solo onomatopoeia explorations contrast their own. "Boing," "slither," and "hush" are good examples of words that provide contrast to each other.

Each ensemble member is responsible for teaching one of their sound-action phrases to the others so that everyone in the ensemble has the same vocabulary: using the preceding example, one "boing" sound action, one "slither" sound action, and one "hush" sound action. Remind students that the three sounds and actions should contrast each other sonically and physically. The levels, direction, timing, use of body, and facial expression should all be different from each other.

Once ensemble members have taught each other their vocabularies, allow ensembles 5 to 10 minutes to create a short movement piece that uses their three contrasting sounds and actions and two pure movement phrases that they create together. Have ensembles present their work, then discuss.

Discussion of Random Factor Variation

- How many ensembles used skills developed in Add Water and Stir in their creation process?
- How important were the pure movement phrases to the pieces?
- How did ensembles create their movement phrases (did they select complementary or contrasting movements to those of their sounds and actions)?
- Did all ensembles perform their pure movement phrases in silence?
- If so, how did the silence affect the pieces?
- Did some of the ensembles create sonics for their movement phrases? If so, how did they select which sounds to use?

SOUND AND BODY ISOLATIONS

Have students select an emotion to communicate through the following isolations:

1. A sound
2. A hand or arm gesture
3. A short traveling movement phrase that uses only the head, torso, legs, and feet (no arms)

Allow students several minutes to work on their own; then, when everyone is ready, ask half the group to find a spot in the performance area and stand in neutral position facing the audience. Look at the group and note similarities and differences in students' clothing and hair. Some may be wearing black tights or short-sleeved T-shirts, some may have their hair pulled back or have bangs, some may have socks on while others are barefoot. This will become important as the exercise progresses.

In the first part of the presentation, everyone works on the same isolation at the same time. Ask all of those performing to present their sounds. Have them vocalize their sounds for approximately 20 seconds. Some may have to repeat their sounds over and over; others may be able to extend their sound for much of the duration. Next, have students present their arm gestures. Have them repeat their gestures for 30 to 45 seconds. Finally, ask them to do their movement phrase. Keep the group working at this for more than a minute, and then ask everyone in the performance group to stop and return to their original spot and stand in neutral.

Now it's time to mix and match. Ask the students in the performance group to note how they are dressed. Tell them that you will now be calling out instructions that will not apply to everyone but will be directed to specific groups of students. For example, you may ask those wearing black tights to do their sounds, those wearing shorts to do only their arms, and those with bare feet to do their movement phrase. Students who fall into more than one of these categories may move from one instruction to another, but only when the new instruction is called out. They may not change activities whenever they wish.

Continue with at least five more changes for the first performance group. Besides clothing, you can use hairstyles, height, jewelry, eye color, freckles, and tattoos. Keep changing the categories so that the audience sees a constant blending of the sounds, hand or arm gestures, and movement phrases. Here are some ideas: Have the people wearing bright-colored T-shirts work their sounds with their backs to the audience. Those wearing shoes combine arm movements and sounds; those with earrings do movement phrases as slowly as possible; those without makeup do their gestural work at center stage. Make sure everyone has the opportunity to perform and observe before starting the discussion.

Discussion

- Could those in the audience identify the emotions the performers were trying to communicate?
- How did having different groups work different isolations at the same time affect what the audience was viewing?
- Was it more interesting than when everyone performed the same isolation at the same time?
- Did the sound isolations work as a soundtrack for those moving in silence?

Random Factor Variation: *Have everyone perform the exercise while holding different props*

Ask students to think of a personal prop that they would like to work with when they repeat this exercise. It might be something relatively small, like a stuffed animal or a book, or it may be larger, like a chair or a broom. Students should pick props that have some connection to the emotion they are communicating.

Students must always be connected (emotionally and physically) to their props. For example, though a student is allowed to jump over her prop during her movement phrase, the prop must never be left lying alone on the floor. She may hold the prop with her hands or with another part of her body, or she may work under and over it. Throwing a small, soft prop up and catching it is fine, but throwing other types of props is too dangerous to be permitted. For safety, remind students to use their peripheral vision while working. Perform the exercise as before and add new categories to call out; for example, those with a fabric prop direct their vocal isolation to their props, and those with wooden props do their traveling isolation toward stage right, and so on.

Discussion of Random Factor Variation

- How did the exercise change with the addition of props?
- Did the exercise now need more or fewer students performing at the same time?
- Were students able to physically and emotionally connect their props to their sounds, gestures, and movement phrases?
- Did the prop add to or detract from any of the three elements?
- Would the exercise work with everyone using the same prop but maintaining their different emotions and isolation elements?

What follows are some journal excerpts from secondary school dance/drama students after participating in dance/drama programming that focused on exploring sound and movement.

- "We learned to analyze the connection between movement and gesture with mood and personal characteristics . . . and how different sounds and actions can reflect and build upon one another. Our week with Janice allowed us to become more self-aware of both external movement and internal physical reactions." —Grade 10 student
- "I was challenged when I had to express a feeling without my body moving at all. . . . I think my physical emotions have grown, I can now show feelings with my body to a much larger range." —Grade 9 student
- "From a personal observation I found that each student was able to express a certain individuality about themselves that no one else could. Not only did we deal with movement, we dealt with sound and expression as well. To sum up everything in a few words I would say that we became individuals." —Grade 10 student

EMphasis, emPHASis, emphasIS

I use a variation of this exercise in technique class when the students are looking emotionally tired and their expression is flat. EMphasis, emPHASis, emphasIS encourages students to explore dynamics in a fun and challenging way.

Have everyone sit in a circle. Offer the group a short phrase or sentence that they are all able to remember and pronounce but that has some rhythmic or sonic challenges. Some examples: "Cinnamon butter on toast," "Linguine again?," and "Uniform units unite us."

Speak the phrase as clearly as possible, then have one student at a time repeat the phrase word for word, but each time the phrase is spoken, there should be a change in the rhythm, vocal level, emphasis of pronunciation, or emotional intent. It may be necessary to remind students that they may not change the actual wording of the phrase. Go around the circle several times without anyone repeating any of the variations that have already been spoken. At first, students will go for the obvious: all the words spoken very quickly or slowly, loudly or softly. The longer you work at this aspect of the exercise, the more interesting the offerings become: "Cin-in-in-in-aaaahhh-mon-on BUTT errrrr? ON toas-Toes! TOES! T."

Approach a simple movement phrase in a similar fashion. Start by demonstrating a movement phrase (e.g., jump twice, shake knees, reach out with the left arm, and drop chin to chest) and pass it around the circle with students emphasizing various elements of the phrase. Explore repetitions, direction changes, weight of attack, dramatic exaggerations, and so forth.

Ask students to create their own word phrase and three variations of that phrase (without changing any of the words). Then ask them to create their own movement phrase and three variations of that phrase (by exploring repetitions, timing, weight, direction, etc.). Then have them put the two phrases together

for presentation. As each person presents their work, you may wish to have him first speak his word phrase clearly and then present his movement phrase clearly so that observers will know the foundation phrases. During presentation of the variations of the text and movement phrases, ask students to speak and move at the same time.

Discussion

- How many students had their actions animate the meaning of their word phrases?
- How many students used abstract movement that did not intentionally relate to their phrases?
- How many students created word phrases that did not follow traditional sentence structure (e.g., "Sky under I walk")?
- Was one style more effective than another?
- Were there any unique ways that students manipulated their phrases?
- Identify the elements that were used in the most successful phrases.

Random Factor Variation: *Eliminate the use of verbs and arm movements*

Give students several minutes to practice their word and movement phrases without speaking any of the verbs in their word phrases or using any arms in their movement phrases. Have students present their work one at a time, first speaking their foundation phrase (without the verbs), then performing their foundation movement phrase (without arms), then performing their three word and movement phrase variations.

Discussion of Random Factor Variation

- Did leaving out the arm movements make the remaining movement phrase more difficult to perform?
- Did leaving out the arm movements make the mover more aware of facial expression, torso, legwork, and footwork?
- Did the word phrase make sense even when the verbs were left out?
- Did the movement phrase tend to imply the action that the verbs represented?
- Did everyone remember that words like "am," "are," "were," and "is" are verbs?
- Did anyone have a word phrase that contained no verbs (e.g., "cinnamon butter and toast") or a movement phrase without arms?

STRANGE BUT TRUE PHRASES

This is one of my favorite exercises for advanced students. Unlike most of the exercises in Poetry and Prose, this one requires a fair amount of creation and rehearsal time. Students really enjoy Strange but True Phrases and create wonderful choreography as a result.

Work with your class to compile a list of commonly used phrases that, when literally interpreted, contain unusual physical descriptions. "Falling head over heels in love," "skip to the facts," "dying to meet you," and "keep your eyes peeled" are just a few of the strange but true phrases that work in this exercise. Print each of the phrases you and your class come up with on individual pieces of paper, fold them so that the text is hidden, and place them in a bag, shoe box, or hat.

Divide the group into small ensembles of three to five students each. One member from each ensemble reaches into the bag and picks a strange but true phrase. Each ensemble must use the phrase that its member selected as the foundation for a silent movement piece.

Encourage ensembles to weave literal gestures with lyrical movement phrases. The movement phrases used in these pieces should be derived from the word phrase's rhythm, emotional content, and specific verbs and actions stated in the phrase. An ensemble working with "falling head over heels in love" may combine several elements: the action of falling, head and heel isolations to attach one person to another, a series of somersaults, and a very beautiful movement phrase that communicates a sense of love and warmth. Text and subtext. Literal and symbolic. Funny, serious, and very human. The end result provides the audience with moving images that touch on a variety of aspects of that unpredictable state called love. Allow students to work for several classes creating and rehearsing their pieces. Have all of the ensembles present their work before discussing the choreography.

Discussion

- Were those in the audience able to guess the phrase each piece was based on?

- Were all ensembles able to combine lyrical and literal interpretations of their phrases in their dance work?

- Which was more difficult, creating the lyrical movement phrase or creating the literal one?

- The dances were all performed in silence. Did performers find themselves counting to themselves, or speaking the phrase in their minds, or a combination of the two in order to keep the timing of the piece?

Random Factor Variation: *Create a sonic collage*

This random factor variation may require out-of-class production time. One can approach this variation in one of two ways: either use sound equipment to build the collage, or ask students to perform it live using their voices and other simple sounds that they can generate without technical support. If recording equipment is available and students are interested, scripting and then recording this random factor can become an exciting multimedia project. A simple, nontechnical way to try this variation is to follow the steps up to scripting, complete the script, and then have students vocalize the script.

Ask ensembles to create a sonic collage for their Strange but True Phrases dance pieces. The collage must incorporate music (elements from any style; e.g., classical, pop, jazz, or world music and any type of sound effects) and text (dialogue, poetry, news reports) but must not contain the actual phrase an ensemble is working on.

For example, the ensemble working with "head over heels in love" may use the theme from the film *Love Story* and Billie Holiday singing "My Man." They can create soap opera–style dialogue ("Oh, John, what's to become of us?" "Martha, I love you. Nothing bad can happen now.") or excerpt lines from Shakespeare's sonnets or plays, or from literature, poetry, even the washroom walls.

If students have the technical sound equipment and skills to record and edit their scripts, give them the time to create a finished tape or CD. This may take several weeks, so remind students to keep rehearsing their choreography. Once the tapes or CDs are finished, ask ensembles to present their pieces with the recorded sonic collage.

For situations where recording the script is not feasible, ask ensembles to perform their scripts live. This can be done in one of three ways. Ensembles can present their sonic collages without movement, they can present their sonic collages while they do their movement, or they can team up with another ensemble and ask the other ensemble to vocalize the sonic collage while they perform their movement.

Discussion of Random Factor Variation

- Did the sonic collage influence the performers' movement and facial expressions?
- Did the performers embrace the emotions more fully in their movement when there was sound?
- Did the sonic collage ever overpower the original movement piece?
- Did all the ensembles choose to take a humorous approach, or did some create sonic collages that explored more serious aspects of their strange but true phrases?
- Discuss and explore other methods of combining spoken text and movement.
- How did creating the collages compare to creating a piece of choreography?

SET TEXT

The exercises in this chapter have helped students explore the various ways in which words and vocalizations can be interpreted through movement. Participants will have discovered that instead of looking just at a word's literal meaning, they should also listen to the sounds and rhythm, the subtext, and the weight of the words or the playfulness in a phrase when responding to it through movement.

Now that students have opened their ears and their bodies to the musical potential of words and phrases, ask them to try memorizing a poem or a short piece of text to use as the foundation for an original piece of choreography. The Set Text structure is most easily described in a recipe format. This allows student ensembles the freedom to create a work that is serious or silly (or both), to include as many technical challenges as they feel they can handle, and to have a true sense of ownership of the piece from start to finish.

Set Text requires a fair amount of creation and rehearsal time. Instruct students to memorize the text before they start to create their choreography.

Set Text required ingredients include the following:

● An ensemble of four or more

● A short piece of writing (which the ensemble members must find and memorize) to be the foundation for the piece

- A purely vocal section in which performers must vocalize words and phrases from the text
- To contrast the vocal section, a purely lyrical movement section consisting of a 24- to 36-beat phrase (this may be performed either in silence or to recorded music; sound effects; or sonic creations, performed by ensemble members, that are different from those used in the purely vocal section)
- A gestural section, featuring exaggerated movements of the arms, face, and upper body
- A section combining the elements of the spoken text, lyrical phrase, and gestural sections

Set Text challenges students to use all the skills they have acquired while working with the poetry and prose exercises in this chapter. The end product can be quite impressive. Students will need time to memorize text, create choreography and vocals, record music, and rehearse.

Discussion

Ask each ensemble about its creative and rehearsal process, focusing on how the members came to choose their text and how they felt about the way they combined the words and movement. Then discuss the individual pieces, starting with the strengths.

- "What was the most memorable moment in each piece?"
- "Why was it memorable?"
- "How did ensembles work the purely vocal sections into their choreography?"
- "Did ensembles find unique ways of integrating text and movement?"
- "Did any of the pieces surprise you by going off in an expected direction?"
- "Did any of the required ingredients force ensembles into sections that they would have been happy to omit?"
- "If yes, what were they, what other required ingredient(s) would you rather have substituted, and why?"

Random Factor Variation: *Create your own random factor variation*

Let the individual ensembles decide in which direction their choreography should travel. Perhaps the final discussion questions will have helped the ensembles identify some of the possible random factors they can explore. Make sure to provide adequate planning and rehearsal time for all of the ensembles to rework their choreography before they present their pieces.

Discussion of Random Factor Variation

After each ensemble presents their work, ask those watching to identify the random factor each ensemble selected. See how many times those in the audience are correct.

- Ask members from each ensemble to explain why they selected their random factor (e.g., to add humor, impose physical limitations, or emphasize a specific element or section).
- Did ensemble members feel that the random factor they selected worked in the way they had hoped?
- Did audience members feel the random factors that ensembles selected made the choreography stronger?
- If you have time to continue working on these pieces, see what happens when ensembles trade their random factor variations. Allow ensembles adequate time for reworking their choreography, then present and discuss.

The challenges students face in Set Text and Strange but True Phrases help to prepare them for the next chapter. All the exercises in that chapter require students to be able to work in ensembles and create original choreography based on a single object or image.

If your students are not disciplined in their rehearsal process or lack the confidence to rely on their own ideas and initiatives, they may not be ready to move on to the exercises in chapter 5. Instead, revisit the recipes in chapter 2, or create your own recipes and assign them in the following order.

- First, have all your students do a recipe that requires them to work on a solo. This helps them gain confidence in themselves, their ideas, and their performance dynamics.
- Then choose a recipe for two or three dancers to help students develop their ability to communicate their ideas and to collaborate and compromise with others.
- Finally, ask students to work in an ensemble recipe for four or more dancers. Help ensembles establish a rehearsal strategy, assigning specific students to oversee specific sections of the choreography so that ensemble members avoid arguments and learn to take on responsibilities. This will help students develop their leadership, production, and organizational skills.

After your students have successfully revisited the recipes, you can move on to objects and images.

5

Objects and Images

*T*he exercise ideas in this chapter offer you and your students a chance to apply all the skills acquired in the earlier chapters with a special focus on exploring aesthetics and translating visual images and personal impressions into movement. Students should be encouraged to keep journals to record objects and images they are personally drawn to. After students have explored all the ideas in this book, they can go to their journals and create works based on their journal entries.

The Concept Behind Objects and Images

All of the exercises in this chapter can be developed into substantial works of choreography. An object or image is presented, discussed, and then translated into movement patterns by individual students who then team up in small ensembles to create large choreographic pieces. Encourage students to commit to rehearsal schedules outside of class time. Production and promotional skills can also be developed if the class wishes to present their pieces in a more formal venue with an invited audience.

Application

Many of the exercises from chapter 1 were based on the way real things moved. Favorite exercises such as Tag and Ping-Pong are based on simple games. Flocking is based on the flying patterns of geese, and Wave Walk is based on the movement of waves on the shore. The subjects that you and your students will explore in this chapter also come from the real world.

While working with props in chapter 3, students manipulated tactile objects. They experienced firsthand how objects can impose limitations on established movement patterns as well as offer a wealth of inspiration for new ways of moving.

Now we ask students to study actual physical structures, discuss and analyze these structures' kinetic and emotional elements, and translate what they have observed into original movement patterns and choreography. With these exercises, you and your class can create in-depth movement pieces using collected impressions and observations of specific images.

Discussion plays a vital role in working with objects and images. Most of the exercises begin with a discussion and, as in the poetry and prose exercises in the last chapter, words, phrases, and ideas from these discussions should be recorded in personal journals or a class notebook and referred to as the movement work develops.

In chapter 2's recipes, students were given a list of required ingredients (specific qualities, timings, shapes, and actions) but were given the freedom to manipulate the required ingredients in any way they wished. Each list of ingredients guided students in their creative assignments by giving them limitations that helped to hold their choreography together. As their confidence grew, students added more and more of their own transitional movement patterns, and the required ingredients became less central to the choreography.

In this chapter students have almost total control. They explore movement ideas and then select the movement patterns they think work best to communicate a given image, determining their own list of required ingredients.

The first two Objects and Images exercises in this chapter explore board games. The next two look at things we frequently handle. Those are followed by two exercises focusing on things we move through, and the final two images explore visual art. All these exercises will challenge students with strong movement vocabularies and those who have an interest in choreography. At the same time, I have been surprised by how many students with no movement background have also excelled at them.

While visiting the small rural community of Gooderham, Ontario (three hours north of Toronto), my partner, Barry, and I taught a music and movement class to a group of students in grades 4, 5, and 6 who had had no previous dance experience. In the first hour I introduced simple movement concepts and led stretching and strengthening exercises to warm everyone up. We had completed several versions of Back to Front, when one of the boys approached me and asked if we could draw squares on the gym floor to create a dance where we assumed the shapes and movements of chess pieces. I was amazed. I told him that I thought it was a great idea, and so did his classmates. In discussion we all agreed that, unfortunately, his idea would take quite a bit of time to accomplish, more time than we had available. I asked if there were any simpler games that we could turn into a dance. Snakes and Ladders (one of my favorite games to analyze and choreograph to with students) was suggested. In the time remaining we discussed the movement qualities of each of the subjects and created substantial movement patterns for "snakes" and "ladders."

Living in the country, these students knew more about both subjects than most urban dwellers, and their observational skills were excellent. Though I had used Snakes and Ladders many times before, I had never had a student suggest horizontal movements for ladders. Normally students focus on vertical and diagonal movements. In Gooderham we made sure our ladders also moved horizontally, because, as one student said, that's how ladders move when you carry them. To fulfill the image of ladders moving horizontally, we did a push-up, held the "up" position, then propelled ourselves backward by pushing off with our hands and the balls of the feet and toes while maintaining a rigid, horizontal torso position and straight legs. We repeated these small hand and toe hops on a fast, even beat for eight counts, then walked our hands toward our feet so that we assumed the inverted *V* of an opened ladder.

Regardless of their technical ability, students can excel at the objects and images exercises. Success in these exercises will depend on good group dynamics, cooperative work habits, and their ability to conceptualize and verbally communicate ideas. Students will require creation time, rehearsal time, and space. Several of the exercises may inspire ensembles to manipulate the presentation space. Some of the random factors will lead you off in a technical direction, which may require preparation and planning time on your part as well as that of the students.

Remind students that it's okay to change or remove sections from a piece, even if they've worked at it for a number of days (they can always put it back in). It's not unusual for choreographers to have to scratch sections of a piece because it just wasn't going in the right direction. At the same time, deadlines must be met. Sometimes students will have to settle for presenting a piece they don't feel completely satisfied with. Make it a learning experience. After all, we learn a lot from our mistakes. Enjoy and benefit from the process, both the failures and the successes.

If you teach dance or drama in a school setting, you may wish to start students on one exercise and allow them two or three weeks to complete and present it, then allow another week or two for them to work with its random factor variation. If you teach at a dance studio and see your students several times a week, you may want to explore one or two of the exercises as a way to further develop students' group compositional skills. You may even wish to use the choreographic ideas yourself for creating recital or performance pieces. If so, use the discussion ideas with your dancers to help them understand the concept behind your choreography. Every class has its own personality and pace, and each teacher has her own schedule. Use as much time as you see fit for these exercises.

TIC-TAC-TOE

Use shapes and movement concepts from the game of tic-tac-toe (also known as Xs and Os) as the foundation for a structured movement exercise or piece of choreography.

Have students find a spot in the room where they can work on their own. Ask them to explore Os, or circles. Allow students to work on their own for several minutes to see how many circular shapes they can make with their bodies. They can work on creating circular shapes with different parts of their bodies or create movement patterns that travel across the floor. Remind students not to forget the vocal work from chapter 4. They may find it helpful to explore circular sounds as they move in a circular fashion.

Ask students to present one or two of their circular movement patterns (with or without sound). After exploring the O shapes and circle sounds and actions, have students explore and then present their ideas for the X shape and crossing movement patterns (with or without sounds).

Discussion

- Identify the five most obvious ways the X and O movement patterns differed.

- Did any of the X or crossing movement patterns have circular aspects? If so, identify (arms "ticking" in a clocklike fashion, flat back "drop swings" may create an arc in the air, etc.).

- Did any of the O or circular movement patterns have X or crossing aspects? If so, identify them (interlocking legs or arms, overlapping footwork pattern, etc.).

- Even though some of the O shapes had X aspects (and vice versa), did students approach Os and Xs with different qualities of attack or performance energy? If yes, identify them.

Random Factor Variation: Change the performance area so that it takes on the appearance of a game board

Now that you and your class have explored some of the movement qualities of Xs and Os, review and discuss the rules and actions used in the actual game of tic-tac-toe. You should identify the following:

- The game is played on a simple grid consisting of two horizontal lines that cross two vertical lines.

- There are two players: one X, one O.

- A player may write an X or an O in any square on the grid that has not been filled.

- The object of the game is to dominate the grid with a connected line of three Xs or Os.

- A straight horizontal, vertical, or diagonal line must connect three of the same letters to win.
- Many games end in a draw.

If students are unfamiliar with the game, have them play it on a chalkboard or on paper so that they can see the *X*s and *O*s on the grid and some of the strategies involved.

The simplest way to turn the performance area into a game board is to place tape on the floor to form the traditional tic-tac-toe grid. Ask students to work in ensembles of six or more to create a tic-tac-toe movement piece using vocabulary developed in the original exercise.

The object of this exercise is to have ensembles structure their movement patterns to fit or complement the grid taped to the floor. They may choose to augment the grid with risers, glow tape, bodies lying on the floor on top of the tape, elastic, rope, or special lighting. Indeed, encourage them to find ways of transforming the performance area into a game board in any way they can. Once they have established how they wish to transform the performance area, they should then apply the *X* and *O* movement vocabulary to discover ways that the opposing forces can interact choreographically.

Students must incorporate the grid pattern into their choreography. Some ensembles may choose to move only on the lines of tape and freeze in the squares. Others may wish to create props that represent the *X*s and *O*s and carry them

out to the performance space, leaving the props in the squares while they fight their battle for grid domination outside the grid.

This, like all of the exercises in this chapter, will take several classes to accomplish, as well as rehearsal time after school. When all of the ensembles are ready, have them present their work and then discuss each ensemble's ideas and creative process as well as the audience's response.

Discussion of Random Factor Variation

- Identify the various ways in which ensembles succeeded in fulfilling the random factor variation of making the performance area into a game board.

- How many ensembles literally recreated a tic-tac-toe game?

- Did any ensembles add emotional or symbolic qualities to their pieces? If yes, what were they?

- Was the tic-tac-toe game still evident in the pieces that added emotional or symbolic interpretations?
- If no ensemble had thought to add emotional or symbolic qualities, discuss the idea now and compile a list of possible ways to go about adding emotional or symbolic qualities to abstract *X* and *O* shapes and movement (e.g., conflicting sides in a war, different cultures, ages, sexes, and so on).

SNAKES AND LADDERS

The first step in exploring this concept is similar to the work done in the previous exercise of Tic-Tac-Toe. As before, you will be using shapes and movement concepts from a board game as a foundation for choreography.

Review the game of Snakes and Ladders so all students know how to play it. For teachers unfamiliar with this simple board game, the rules are as follows:

- It's for two to eight players.
- Players place their men at the starting position at the bottom square of a game board similar to a chess board, except for the fact that snakes and ladders of various lengths have been diagonally placed across many of the squares.
- Players roll dice to determine how many squares their men can move each time their turn comes up.
- The men travel horizontally across the board, from square to square; their ultimate goal is to reach the uppermost square at the top left corner of the board.
- If a player lands on a square containing the lowest rung of a ladder, the player gets to climb up the ladder, putting him at a higher position on the board.
- If a player lands on a square containing the head of a snake, the player must slide down the snake, putting him at a lower position on the board.
- All of the snakes and ladders are different lengths, making some snakes very dangerous and some ladders very advantageous.
- The first player to arrive at the last square in the upper left corner of the board wins.

Discuss with your class the various ways the snake movement in the game contrasts with the movement of the ladders.

- Down versus up
- Slide versus climb
- Fall versus rise

Discuss with your class the various ways the snake movement in the game contrasts emotionally from the movement of the ladders.

- Failure versus success
- Punishment versus reward

In what ways do snakes and ladders differ in the real world?

- Snakes are living beings; ladders are not.
- Snakes can move by their own power; ladders are manipulated by outside forces.

- Snakes are supple and elastic; ladders are relatively solid and set.
- Snakes can be predators and be preyed upon; ladders can be bought and sold, borrowed and broken.

Ask your class to work on their own, with half the students exploring ways of translating the snake ideas into movement and half exploring ways of translating the ladder ideas into movement. After approximately five minutes of exploration, ask students to create and memorize a 16- to 24-beat movement phrase that communicates aspects of the snake or the ladder, depending on which one they had been previously exploring. In another five minutes students should be ready to present their work.

Discussion

- Did all of the snake movement phrases contain the same qualities?
- Identify any surprising, unique, or unusual ways students interpreted the snake.
- Did all of the ladder movement phrases contain the same qualities?
- Identify any surprising, unique, or unusual ways students interpreted the ladder.
- Identify the ways the snake and ladder movement phrases contrasted each other.

Random Factor Variation: *Have one movement pattern overwhelm and transform another*

Ask each student whose movement pattern explored snakes to pair up with a student whose movement pattern explored ladders. Together, the two create a new movement piece in which the two original movement patterns start off as equals, but one of the two patterns overpowers the other and becomes dominant.

You may wish to have students first experiment with their movement patterns before they plan their pieces. A fun way to do this is to have pairs start at opposite sides of the room, then move toward each other using their movement phrases. Once they meet, the pairs repeat their patterns beside and around each other several times. Remind students that while they are doing their own pattern, they should also be responding to the other person's movements. They should be noticing the other person's levels (high or low), tempos (slow or fast), directions (faces only one direction or faces all directions), and attack (moves with soft or sharp accent). This is similar to the random factor variation applied to Ping-Pong in chapter 1.

After several minutes of this, let students go off with their partners and start to set their duets. The pieces they create should not be too long or too complicated. Unlike most of the exercises in this chapter, the application of the random factor for Snakes and Ladders should not require more than 15 to 20 minutes.

Discussion of Random Factor Variation

Once all of the pairs have performed, discuss the following.

- Did one quality (snake or ladder) became the dominant pattern in most of the movement pieces? If yes, which one did, and why? (Did one pattern always have more flexibility in direction or speed? Did one pattern seem to lack outward movement?)
- Did pairs find unique ways to erode one movement pattern and transform it into the other? If yes, identify these ways (e.g., their original patterns shared a similar arm movement that became the key to the transition; one movement pattern was so much faster and more complex than the other that it exhausted itself while the slow, simple pattern was strong and focused throughout).
- Ask pairs to explain their process and discuss any variations they tried before they came up with their final choice.
- Could this variation work for a large ensemble, or is it best kept as a duet?

DAILY CHORES

Start this exercise with a class discussion in which you compile a list of daily chores and mundane activities. This list could include washing dishes, sweeping the floor, cooking, walking to school, cleaning out the litter box, ironing, doing homework, taking out the garbage, shoveling snow, and so on. Ask students to select one of these activities, then have everyone find a spot in the room where they can work on their own.

First ask students to mentally focus on the activity they have chosen—to see and feel the weight of the objects they may be handling, the environment they would be in while doing the chore, the time of day, and so on. Then ask them to perform that activity on the spot (or traveling through the room, as long as they do not interfere with others). Students should truly involve themselves in the activity and put forth as much effort as they would if they were actually doing it. Allow the class two or three minutes of thoughtful, focused work.

After three minutes ask them to do the same activity but try working it on unusual levels (e.g., doing homework standing up or walking with one's back on the floor and legs moving in the air), with unusual combinations (e.g., shaving the floor), with different body parts (e.g., brushing your hair with your elbow or knee), or by drastically changing the timing (e.g., taking 60 seconds to cut a single slice in a vegetable) or size (e.g., writing in a notebook that is half the size of the room). Encourage students to explore a number of these variations. After several minutes of exploration, have students present three of the variations they have discovered.

Discussion

- How did students feel when they first had to do the chore in the normal way?
- If some students say they found it boring, ask why.
- If some students found it interesting, ask why.
- How did students feel about performing the same activity when they were asked to change the levels, timing, and the like?

Many students say that the activity takes on a life of its own, that it's no longer boring because you don't feel like you're doing the same thing over and over again. Other students may argue that you are still doing the same thing over and over again, but you're having to think about it more because you're using different body parts, timings, levels, and so on.

Random Factor Variation: *Create a 12- to 24-beat movement phrase that can be repeated five different ways*

The common thread to all of the chores and daily activities we are working with in this exercise is that in everyday life we repeat them over and over again.

Spend a few minutes discussing examples of how doing the same chore can be a pleasure sometimes and a burden at other times. For example, in the winter you can shovel snow every day for weeks. You may enjoy shoveling snow at night, when the stars are out, the streets are quiet, and the snow is fresh. On the other hand, you may hate having to shovel snow in the morning when you're just waking up, the snowplows have piled up mounds of dirty snow from the street into your driveway, the snow on the sidewalk has been packed down by the heavy boots of passersby, and you know you're going to be late for work.

Notice how the same chore can sound and feel so different? Even the physical action changes: the snow feels light at night, heavy in the morning. The weight of attack, the level of the torso, the bend in the knees, the speed of the action, and even the space around the body doing the shoveling changes from open and spacious at night to compressed and crowded in the morning.

Ask students to go into small ensembles of three to five and first create a 12- to 24-beat movement phrase based on a single chore or daily activity. Then ask ensembles to manipulate that phrase using ideas they developed in the first part of the exercise to create five variations. Finally, give ensembles enough time to incorporate their five phrase variations into a short piece of choreography that contains transitional movement patterns that are not part of their 12- to 24-beat phrase. Then have them present their creations.

Discussion of Random Factor Variation

- Identify the various ways ensembles manipulated their 12- to 24-beat phrase (e.g., no person worked the phrase in unison with another, all worked at different levels, the size of the objects they were manipulating varied from minute to enormous).
- How many pieces communicated a sense of humor?
- How many pieces communicated a sense of despair?
- Where else do simple everyday actions become a vehicle for comedy and tragedy (show students videos of some of the great silent comedy stars— e.g., Laurel and Hardy, Buster Keaton, Charlie Chaplin)?

- Did the audience have a sense of shifting time and space as described in the snow shoveling example? If so, identify the shifting elements and how they were portrayed.
- Spend some time discussing the use of repetition as a choreographic tool.

KNOTS

Start this exercise with a class discussion on the nature of knots, and compile the following lists:

- A list of the positive aspects of knots (they help hold things together)
- A list of their negative aspects (when you can't undo your shoelaces)
- A list of things that get knotted (hair, wood, vines, lives, etc.)
- A list of "knotty" terms (e.g., lover's knots, sailor's knots) and famous phrases ("Oh, what a tangled web we weave . . ." from Shakespeare's *Macbeth*)

To begin the movement segment, have students find a spot in the room where they can work on their own. Ask them to explore ways of tying themselves into knots, such as by twisting the legs, arms, neck, toes, and torso. After a minute or two, ask them to select a knot for themselves that they feel they can hold without too much difficulty.

Once everyone is in their knots, have students explore ways of traveling across the floor while maintaining their twisted shapes. Remind them that they can move by any method (rolling, hopping, dragging, etc.), at any level or variety of levels (e.g., moving up and down like an inchworm), and at any timing (some may manage to move across the entire room in the same time that others cover only inches). Ask students to select one of their ways of moving, and have them present their "traveling knots" in groups of three or four.

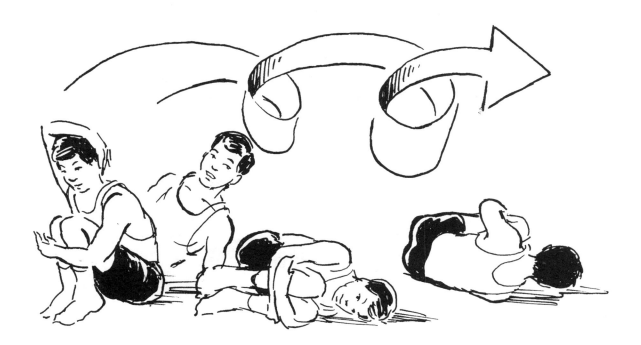

Discussion

- Did any of the traveling knots communicate any of the ideas and images from the lists compiled at the start of the exercise?

- Identify those that did and the reasons that those traveling knots embodied one of the ideas in the lists. For example, did the spiderlike way someone looked make people think of the "tangled web" quotation, or did the hopping on one foot remind everyone of a sailor's jig?

Random Factor Variation: *Maintain only half the required shape*

Ask students to work on their own and modify the traveling knot they created. They now need to keep only half of their original shape, so traveling and working movement combinations can become much easier. Ask students to use the freedom their bodies have to help communicate a specific "knotty" concept. They may use ideas from the lists compiled at the beginning of the exercise or other concepts that come to mind, including "untangling" phrases such as "straighten up" or "clean up your act." By employing contrasting or "untangling" imagery, students often create pieces in which their "knotted" self is struggling with its "unknotted" self. Allow students time to create these short solos, and then have them present their work one at a time.

Discussion of Random Factor Variation

- Did most students choose to free their legs and feet and keep the knot in the upper halves of their bodies?
- Were the concepts behind each of the solos clear?
- Did a number of students pick similar knot concepts?
- Did any of the students use concepts that had not been on the lists (e.g., tossing and turning and waking up tangled in the sheets, Boy Scouts)?
- Would some of these "knotty" concepts be more effectively communicated in an ensemble piece?

Have students go into small ensembles of three to five, select one of the knot concepts, and develop it into a movement piece. Students need not maintain knotted shapes all the time. Now that they have a number of bodies to work with, students should explore ways of moving through each other, connecting themselves to each other, and possibly building a large knotted mass at one point in their piece. Present and discuss.

REVOLVING DOORS

Begin this exercise with a class discussion that focuses on revolving doors. Ask students the following questions:

- "What exactly do revolving doors do?" (Move large numbers of people in and out of buildings faster than other doors; retain the indoor environment more effectively.)
- "Where are they most often found?" (Large office buildings and department stores.)
- "Can everyone use revolving doors?" (They are not accessible for people using wheelchairs, walkers, or strollers.)
- "What are they made of?" (Most often glass and metal; you can see who is revolving with you.)
- Ask as well for personal stories students may have about first seeing a revolving door, playing with them, being trapped in one, or rescuing someone from one.

Ask students to go into ensembles of four or more. Ask half the ensembles to create a 24- to 36-beat movement piece that illustrates the positive aspects of revolving doors. Ask the other ensembles to create a 24- to 36-beat movement phrase that illustrates the negative aspects of revolving doors. Have all the ensembles present.

Discussion

- Identify the textures or movement qualities ensembles used that communicated the positive aspects of revolving doors (e.g., smooth, swift, circular, orderly).

- Identify the textures or movement qualities ensembles used that communicated the negative aspects of revolving doors (e.g., resistance, pressure, irregular speeds).

- Identify similarities found in the positive and negative ensembles (e.g., turning or spinning on the spot, other people interacting with those spinning).

- Did any ensemble apply movement vocabulary from the Tic-Tac-Toe exercise in their choreography?

Random Factor Variation: *Create new ensembles by mixing members from contrasting ensembles*

Ask each ensemble of four to divide itself into two groups of two. Then ask each group of two to team up with a group of two from a different ensemble to form a new ensemble of four. These new ensembles must have two people from an ensemble that explored the positive aspects of revolving doors and two people from an ensemble that explored the negative aspects of revolving doors.

Ask these new ensembles to combine their positive and negative movement phrases to create a more in-depth dance piece. Students may manipulate the positive and negative movement phrases in any way they choose. Ensemble members should start by teaching each other their phrases, then discuss how to manipulate those phrases so that they complement or contrast each other, or both. New transitional phrases can be added. Be sure you discuss with your class just how long you want these pieces to be. This project can be done with relative speed (20 to 30 minutes at its simplest), or it can be developed over several classes.

Discussion of Random Factor Variation

After the new ensembles have presented their work, ask students the following:

- What dynamic or dramatic similarities were present in all the ensembles? Identify and discuss. (Perhaps three moved using positive actions and only one used the negative. Ensembles may have chosen to do this because they believe the majority of people find revolving doors beneficial and easy to use. Is this true?)
- Were there two ensembles that worked with the same movement phrases (i.e., had members from the same original negative and positive groups)? If so, did the two ensembles create similar or contrasting pieces?
- Did any ensemble manipulate its movement phrases in a unique way? If yes, discuss what the ensemble did and ask its members about their creative process.
- If no ensemble manipulated its movement phrases in a unique way, why not? Suggest to students that the revolving door movement can transform into other things: a merry-go-round, washing machine, or bathtub drain; the emotions of confusion or anxiety; an element in nature such as a tornado or whirlpool. Children like to play in revolving doors because it's like riding a merry-go-round; business people running in and out of offices every day become like rats running on the wheels in their cages. The revolving door image can be used as a metaphor for a number of things.

CORRIDORS

Lead a group discussion that focuses on corridors. In these collective discussions you gather important information that will help everyone focus on the nature of the objects being studied. When leading these sessions, you may want to assign note takers and use flip charts if they are available.

One way to stimulate discussion is to work with contrasts. Ideas you should touch on include the following:

- Noisy, crowded corridors versus empty and echoing corridors
- Underground versus above-ground corridors
- Human-made corridors of concrete, tile, or glass verses natural corridors of thick foliage and rocks
- Political and economic corridors like border checkpoints, no-man's-land, and the Iron Curtain
- Mythical corridors, such as the labyrinth on ancient Minos where the Minotaur lived.

Ask students to contribute an image of a corridor from their past (e.g., being wheeled down a hospital corridor before surgery, walking down the corridor on

the first day of school, walking up the stairs to your apartment during an electrical blackout). How do the corridor experiences differ from the revolving door stories? Do the corridor stories contain a stronger emotional or sonic element than the revolving door experiences? If so, students should include those elements in the movement exercises they are about to create.

Ask students to create a corridor recipe. Required ingredients may include a specific sound that increases and diminishes in volume and frequency; a repeated gesture that unifies all of the movers; the use of levels, stage areas, or both to create divisions or "walls" between the movers. Ask students to write their corridor recipe on a piece of paper, then fold that piece of paper and place it in a container (hat, box, bag, etc.).

After everyone has placed their corridor recipes in the container, shake or stir it to mix up the papers. Have students go into small ensembles of three to five, then invite one person from each ensemble to pick a recipe from the container. Any ensemble that picks a recipe one of its members has written must choose another. Allow enough time for ensembles to create and prepare their corridor recipes—this may take several classes—then ask students to present their work.

Discussion

- Did ensembles present a mixed array of corridors, or did the pieces all seem to communicate the same type of corridor?
- Which corridors contrasted each other the most, and why (one was spacious, one was cramped, one group used a lot of solos, another worked mostly in unison)?
- Did the people who wrote the corridor recipes recognize their ideas?
- Were the people who wrote the corridor recipes surprised by any of the ensembles' interpretations? If yes, why?
- Read all of the original corridor recipes aloud (even those that were not picked) and compare the required ingredients. Discuss any unusual required ingredient and see if ensembles wish to add any new ingredients to their work.

Random Factor Variation: Turn off the overhead lights and use handheld flashlights to illuminate the movement, or set spotlights to illuminate certain areas the movements pass through

Take some time to discuss lighting ideas, including the following:

- How to work with handheld flashlights (adjusting dance movements)
- Who should hold the flashlights (when to light oneself or another)
- Whether the flashlights should ever move independently of the dance
- Where spotlights can be used

After ensembles have put their lighting ideas in place, ask them to present their pieces again.

Discussion of Random Factor Variation

- Did the lighting change the space the dancers were moving through? If yes, how?
- How did the lighting change the emotion and the dramatic tension?
- Was each of the ensembles affected by the lighting in the same way?
- In what other ways did the flashlights affect the presentations?
- How did it feel to perform the choreography in this style of lighting?
- As performers, did students feel more exposed or more hidden working in small spots of light?
- Did using the flashlights stimulate any other lighting ideas?

TOTEM POLES

Totem poles are an extraordinary marriage of nature's strength (the tree) and humankind's artistry (the carving). Ask students to research the traditions of the totem pole—the people who carve them, the animals and spirits represented, current artists who carve traditional totem poles, and current artists who apply those traditions to the creation of new forms of Native American art.

Once students have learned a little of the history of totem poles (and possibly other related totemic art forms), have the class discuss the totem pole as a structure to be used for dance. Ask them what required ingredients a movement piece based on totem structures would demand. The list should include the following:

- Levels
- Interlocking bodies
- Images that contrast and complement
- Movement patterns that are unique to individual dancers
- Animated faces
- An underlying force connecting the dancers

Have students go into small ensembles of three to five and develop a movement piece that fulfills all of the preceding required ingredients. This may take several classes, and even after-class rehearsal time. When students are ready, have them present their work to each other.

Discussion

- Did all of the ensembles manage to include all of the required ingredients in their pieces?

- Which required ingredient was the most difficult to translate into movement?

- Identify the different ways in which ensembles translated the ingredient of an underlying force connecting the dancers (music/rhythm, a movement pattern, or a frozen shape/stillness are usually the most common).

Random Factor Variation: *Project slides or hand-painted transparencies on students' work*

Discuss the types of images you might want to project. (You will need at least one slide or overhead projector and a studio or auditorium that has enough depth for the projector to operate a good distance from the dancers so the images cover the majority of the performance area.)

- Slides of Native American art (traditional and contemporary)
- Work by non-native artists who have been influenced by Native American art (Emily Carr is a wonderful example)
- Images of trees: bare, leafy, old, young; solitary city trees, rural forested areas
- Other images of nature: water, rocks, the earth, animals

You can also create your own images by either hand painting clear gels and cutting them to fit viewfinders, or hand coloring sheets of transparencies for use on an overhead projector.

Let each ensemble be responsible for gathering or creating the slides or transparencies they want projected on them during the performance of their piece. Have ensemble members determine the order and timing for the slides or transparencies, then write the order out on a sheet of paper so the job of projecting the images can be handled by someone from another ensemble. Once all the ensembles are ready, ask them to present their work.

Discussion of Random Factor Variation

- Did all the ensembles use the same types of images?
- If yes, how could ensembles expand their image bank to make the visual component of their pieces more original?
- What were the differences in the ways the ensembles utilized their images (timing, repetition, juxtaposition of images, size, etc.)?
- Did the images intensify the choreography or overpower it?
- How is working with the projections similar to working with music?
- If students tried the Corridors exercise, how did using projected images differ from working with the flashlights?

OBJETS D'ART

The last objects and images exercise is completely up to your students. They will be creating solos using an image in art that they find appealing.

Ask students to select a piece of art they would like to use as a foundation for creating choreography. It can be a painting, a sculpture, a weaving, a quilt, ceramics, an illuminated manuscript, a mask, or a piece of jewelry. Have students bring in a photograph, a postcard, or a picture photocopied from a book of the *objets d'art* they have selected, then do a little show-and-tell.

Show-and-tell works best with everyone sitting in a circle. One by one, students present the photographs of their *objets d'art,* and, while each photo is being passed around, the presenting student gives two or three reasons that she thinks it would translate well into dance. Write down those reasons so they can be referred to at a later date.

Some students can spend an eternity working on their solos. Before students start to work, predetermine the minimum and maximum length of a piece. This will differ from class to class depending on the students' age and technical level, the teaching environment (studio or school), and the availability of rehearsal space. During class time allow students to work on their solos in silence. You may also wish to establish an after-school rehearsal schedule, when individuals can work with whatever sonic accompaniment they choose.

Once students are ready, have them present their solos. I like to have three or four students present their solos one after another, then have a class discussion. If the pieces are short, I may ask another three or four students to present, after which we would have another discussion. More than two discussion sessions per class can be a bit overwhelming. Often the presentations can take a number of days. This may mean that some students get considerably longer time to work on their solos than others. You may wish to address this when students present their solos with the random factor variation by reversing the original presentation order.

Discussion

Make sure students have the photographs of their *objets d'art* available for reference in the discussion.

- To initiate discussion of the solo, read aloud two reasons that the student selected her *objet d'art* (as recorded during the show-and-tell at the beginning of the exercise).

- Does the soloist still feel that those reasons were of prime importance to the dance?

- If not, what new elements have taken precedence?

- Did those watching feel that the soloist's original reasons for wanting to translate the *objet d'art* came through in the choreography?

- Looking at the photograph, are there any glaring omissions in the choreography? For example, if the photograph is of a fountain, did the soloist leave out references to water? If it's an illuminated manuscript, are references to text missing?

- Ask the soloist why she chose to omit those references, and discuss audience ideas for incorporating them.

Random Factor Variation: *Create a costume that turns part of the body into a piece of art*

Students can re-create or interpret any part of their *objets d'art* in any material (fabric, papier-mâché, paper, branches, feathers, Styrofoam, wire, etc.) and in any scale (to wear on the fingers, a limb, the torso, the face, or the entire body).

Much of this random factor variation can become an out-of-class assignment. Before students start work on the design and construction of their costume or body art, introduce them to some examples of costume art.

Sculptor Isamu Noguchi created some of Martha Graham's most daring sets and headdresses. Martha Graham's autobiography, *Blood Memory* (Doubleday), and Ernestine Stodelle's biography *Deep Song* (Schirmer) contain wonderful photographs of Noguchi's work. Another excellent resource is Martin Friedman's *Hockney Paints the Stage* (Abbeville Press). This book contains David Hockney's notes, rough sketches, and completed designs for eight operas and dance works. Twentieth-century artists such as Pablo Picasso and Alexander Calder have also designed sets and costumes for modern dance. The German contemporary artist Rebecca Horn has created an amazing collection of body art. (A retrospective of her work was held at the Guggenheim in New York City in 1993. An impressive catalogue was produced to celebrate that exhibition. It is distributed by Rizzoli International Publications, New York.)

Encourage students to look at books on aboriginal dance forms and art: the magical transforming masks of the West Coast Native Americans, the delicate finger puppets of the Inuit people, and the intricate tattoos of the Maori. The classical dance forms of India, Indonesia, Bali, China, and Japan have for centuries integrated storytelling, music, dance, mask, and puppetry to create some of the world's most spectacular performing art traditions.

Set a time limit on the project. Discourage students from getting too elaborate. Remind them that the costume or body art they create for themselves must be worn throughout their dances, so lightness and durability are important elements to consider. Students must design and construct something that is strong enough to withstand the wear and tear of rehearsal without causing wear and tear on their bodies.

Have students present their solos (limit the number of presenters per day, as suggested in the original exercise) with their costumes or body art. At the end of each class, discuss the works that were presented.

Discussion of Random Factor Variation

Ask individual dancers the following questions:

- "How did you decide on your costume or body art design (the art itself, the placement on the body, the materials used, etc.)?"
- "Did your relationship to your choreography change once you were wearing the costume or body art?"
- "Did your relationship to the *objet d'art* that was your original inspiration change as you created and rehearsed in the costume or body art?"

Ask the audience the following questions:

- "Did the costume or body art complement the original choreography? If so, how? If not, why not?"
- "Did you spend more time watching the part of the body wearing the costume or body art than the rest of the dancer's body?"
- "Was there a more obvious sense of time, place, or emotion in the presentation with the costume or body art than when it was originally performed?"

Dancers are drawings, paintings, mobiles, masks, and sculptures come to life. When we choreograph and perform, we become the artist and the art.

The list of objects and images that you can use as a foundation for choreography and theatrical movement pieces is limitless. Take the time to look, and you'll find yourself noticing movement patterns in everything. After working with me on a four-day program last spring, one elementary school teacher said, "I can't believe I never noticed these patterns before. They're everywhere, and now I just stop and stare. I'm seeing the world in a whole new way."

chapter 6

Dancescape Projects

Students learn how to translate environmental information, computer technology, or visual art into movement pieces. In some projects, students collect information by employing academic research skills, journal writing, sound recording, and photography. The movement pieces created in these projects lead students to a better understanding of their environment, themselves, technology, and visual art.

The Concept Behind Dancescapes

As infants we are fascinated by our everyday surroundings. As we grow up, however, we become so familiar with our surroundings that we stop looking and thinking about the things around us. Students study different environments at school to gain knowledge and understanding of the world, but they must wait years before they can actually apply that knowledge. Too often it gets filed away as yet another fact that was memorized but never put to use.

Choreographers observe their environments. Since earliest times we humans have studied the living things around us and created dances to celebrate their existence and our relationship to them. Modern choreographers continue this tradition. We look to geographic, technological, political, and emotional environments for inspiration in creating new works.

Dancescape projects give students the opportunity to combine their academic studies with their movement work. This chapter documents four very different dancescape projects for classroom use. Two of these projects introduce students to movement concepts, develop basic dance skills, and use observations of natural and human-made environments as the foundation for choreography. The other two projects describe ways to combine movement studies with other art forms (visual art and music) and technology (computer graphics).

Movement and Environmental Studies: Beachscape Project

The first beachscape project took place in the autumn of 1983 at Kew Beach Public School in the City of Toronto. The school is located near the shores of Lake Ontario. Immediately behind the school is a large park, and to the south of the park is a long boardwalk and beach.

I worked with 24 fifth- and sixth-grade students for a total of 40 hours. Very few of the students had had previous movement experience. I visited the school two days a week, two hours each visit, for 10 weeks. During the first two weeks I introduced students to dance and dramatic movement fundamentals. Students were given notebooks to record the exercises along with their feelings about the movement work, their life at home, and their neighborhood environment. Journals help students develop their writing and observation skills. I always tell students that I will be looking at their journals throughout the project. Most often I take them home for review midway through a project. Reading their comments and observations helps me evaluate my own effectiveness; in addition, students get to share some of their unspoken thoughts.

In the third week I shortened the technique classes and began taking students out to the park and beach to observe the environment. Before each outing I assigned specific things for them to observe and write about in their journals. I encouraged the students to do factual documentation, sketching, and creative writing.

Students studied the variety of ground textures—grass, rock, and sand—and the contrasts and similarities between water, earth, and sky. We observed people on the boardwalk: the elderly, young mothers pushing strollers, and dog walkers being pulled quickly by. We spent a cold, windy afternoon sitting out on the rocks getting splashed by the waves. To keep warm we clapped out a rhythm as, one by one, we called out adjectives or adverbs that described an aspect of water. When we finished, everyone had to write a short piece that utilized the vocabulary we had learned. Another day we collected driftwood, rocks, smooth and shiny glass fragments, seaweed, and odd jetsam for original sculptures that we built in the sand.

We recorded all of these activities in our journals and on film. We viewed the slides and used our general arts vocabulary to discuss the images. After two weeks of outings I told the students that it was time for us to start translating our observations into movement pieces. "How?" was their response. "Well," I said, "before we can do this we have to understand more thoroughly what we observed."

This meant that students had to research the environmental activities they had observed. We gathered pages of facts about wind and water, about why leaves change color in autumn and fall from the trees. We studied the migrating habits of various birds, and learned why some birds have stopped migrating and how that has changed the environment. Much of this was done as homework, with students presenting their findings after the technique portion of the movement class. After two weeks we started to use this information as a foundation for choreography.

Beachscape Project in Action

Students used the following movement exercises from the earlier chapters in this book to translate their beachscape observations into movement pieces.

How We Used Wave Walk

Wave Walk is based on the way waves travel up onto the beach and then recede, sometimes leaving behind objects on the sand. First students performed the exercise as it is described in chapter 1 (see page 10). Once they had achieved perfectly straight lines and smooth transitions from frozen shapes to action, I asked students to suggest how we could make the exercise communicate more waterlike qualities. The immediate response was that the walking was too controlled. Water, they said, can be calm and smooth, but it also races onto the shore and crashes into rocks.

The students had just identified the choreographic tools we needed to manipulate: timing and attack. So first we played with the speed of the line as it moved across the stage. Students walked, ran, and leaped across the stage. We created movement phrases that incorporated different levels and qualities of

attack. Students used peripheral vision and counted the beats of the combinations to maintain the straight lines. One combination included jumps, turns, rolls, and lunges with wild arms. It really captured the anger of the lake during a storm. Another combination worked triplets and body swings that undulated gently. It beautifully illustrated the soothing and tranquil qualities of the lake. We worked a canon with several lines starting at different times to show the endless pattern of wave upon wave upon wave on the shore. When students assumed the frozen shapes, they let themselves be pulled, dragged, and eroded each time the waves went by. We played a variety of different types of music, from Indonesian gamelan to contemporary works by Philip Glass and Lou Harrison to environmental water sounds. We also experimented with projecting the slides we had taken of the lake on the upstage wall while we danced.

How We Used Flocking

The Flocking exercise is based on the flight pattern of Canadian geese, native to the shores of Lake Ontario. I introduced students to the simplest form of Flocking as described in chapter 1 of this book (see page 23). Then students worked on their own, finding ways to take the flock format and make it illustrate contrasting aspects of the park and beach environment.

First we had to identify the choreographic tools we could use. Flocking needs to be performed slowly to be successful, so we agreed that we couldn't rely on speed to show contrasts. Instead, students relied heavily on levels and shapes to communicate their ideas. The most successful adaptation was a simple variation based on triple flocking. Three flocks of four went into overlapping flock formation. One group represented air, one earth, one water. Each flock limited itself to shapes and levels that best communicated the living things and textural qualities of its specific element. The air flock worked the upper levels, doing careful balance work and slow traveling steps throughout the stage area, moving slowly through the other two flocks. The water flock worked low and medium levels and explored shifting of weight and smooth, liquid actions, never leaving its original spot. The earth flock did two things. It moved incredibly slowly, working the lowest level, and then it became living things, moving more freely and interacting with the other flocks.

How We Used Tag

Have you ever watched Canadian geese while they feed on dry land? All the birds in the entire flock pluck at the grass with their heads down, except for two or three birds that act as sentries, walking through the flock, ready to call out a warning in case of attack. These guard geese don't patrol forever, however. When they are tired or hungry, they peck a feeding goose, and without argument, the two switch roles. The Tag exercise in chapter 1 (see page 14) is quite similar.

I asked students what choreographic tools we would need to use to make the Tag exercise express our observations of how the geese feed. They identified action, emotion, and timing as being the tools. So instead of having frozen shapes scattered throughout the performance area, students found a spot on the floor and performed simple, repeatable patterns based on grooming or eating with exaggerated slowness. Then I touched three students, who started to travel through the stage area. They used movements that communicated caution, and their arm movements and facial expressions showed that they were looking for something. They explored a variety of levels and timings. After 20 seconds it was time for those three to pass the movement on. After touching someone, each of the three assumed a simple, on-the-spot eating or grooming pattern, while the students they had touched assumed the cautious movement work across the stage.

How We Used EMphasis, emPHASis, emphasIS and Soundtracks

We used the vocabulary of adjectives and adverbs that we had accumulated at the beach in a fashion very similar to that used in the EMphasis, emPHASis, emphasIS exercise from chapter 4 (see page 102). First we reviewed the vocabulary while sitting in a circle, using the clapping rhythm and calling out the word "water" before each new word. It sounded like this: "Water splashes, water bubbles, water churns, water ripples, water freezes, water glistens, water crashes, water melts, water falls . . ."

Students then selected two words they felt illustrated contrasting qualities. Working on their own and using their voices as sonic accompaniment, individuals created three different movement phrases for each of their words. Then they connected all of the phrases together so that each person had a compact solo. After we viewed the solos, we looked for a way to fit them together into a performance piece. The vocal work became the key, and we found the Soundtracks exercise from chapter 4 helpful (see page 91). Half the class worked in the stage area while the others watched. Students onstage performed their solos one at a time, with the offstage students calling, whispering, and singing the words the soloist had used.

Here are some excerpts from journals the students kept that year:

- "It is a very cold and windy day. The leaves blow in my face. It feels as though I am going to fly away with the leaves! I wonder what it would be like?"
- "On the beach, in the sand. I hold a million rocks here in my hand."
- "Water hitting rocks on the beach,
  Wind smacking people's faces,
  Sticks lying in unkept sand,
  People kissing on the shore,
  Windy, sunny and cool!"

Dramatic Movement, Self, and Society: Urbanscape

The first Urbanscape project took place in the spring of 1984 at St. Joseph's College in downtown Toronto. St. Joseph's College, an all-girls secondary school, is less than a five-minute walk from the provincial government buildings, the University of Toronto, several hospitals, and the Royal Ontario Museum. It is also

less than five minutes away from Yonge Street, which is home to shopping centers, theaters, restaurants, strip clubs, pinball arcades, head shops, panhandlers, and kids living on the streets.

I worked with one class of 11th-grade drama students for five weeks, visiting the school three times a week for two-and-a-half hours at a time. This was their third year of dramatic studies. They were comfortable doing improvisational work, and Susan Wilson, their drama teacher, had just completed a section on mime. This project was viewed as a continuation of communicating ideas using nonverbal performance skills.

We started out doing dance technique classes and creative movement exercises from chapter 1 of this book. Students began to keep journals, recording their families' patterns (mealtime, bedtime, weekends, etc.), their daily travel patterns to school (few students lived within walking distance; most took buses or the subway), and their thoughts and feelings about the movement class and their lives in general. After two weeks we compared notes and found these recurring images.

- What it's like traveling on the subway, buses, streets, and sidewalks at rush hour
- Students sneaking off at lunchtime to the pinball arcades on Yonge Street or skipping class and going to the park behind the Parliament buildings
- Argumentative, humorous, or boring family get-togethers
- Tedious daily necessities such as doing laundry and homework

We had a great time laughing and commiserating over the journal entries. We agreed that there were four obvious areas to focus our work on, and we decided to call the recurring themes "Rush Hour," "Family Celebrations," "Escapes," and "The Daily Grind." During the remaining weeks of the project, we used these themes to create dramatic movement and modern dance pieces.

Urbanscape in Action

The following movement exercises from the earlier chapters of this book helped students translate their observations into movement pieces.

How We Used Chairs

We used the Chairs exercise to help establish environments for "Family Celebrations" and "The Daily Grind." For "The Daily Grind" we explored the suggestions listed in Chairs in chapter 3 (see page 63). Five Times Five with chairs was very successful (and we used seven shapes). Instead of communicating their own daily grinds, students portrayed the office workers they rubbed shoulders with every morning during rush hour. They limited themselves to positions office workers might assume throughout the course of a day, with the exception of two of the shapes. Those remaining shapes used the chair in an exaggerated or "over the top" fashion: they held it overhead, huddled underneath it, and so on. Students repeated their five ordinary shapes a number of times, holding the shapes for fewer and fewer beats. The two exaggerated shapes were not included until the speed reached a frantic pace; after 30 frenetic seconds of office worker mayhem, the timing gradually slowed to the original tempo, and the two exaggerated shapes were excluded. As the piece developed, students animated their shapes by moving a body part (e.g., fingers moving over a keyboard, arm tossing paper into the garbage; for the exaggerated shapes, knees shaking and eyes rolling while hiding under the chair, lifting the chair overhead and lowering it while bending the knees). I selected the Steve Reich composition "Drumming, Part 1" as the score; this added an extra element of tension to the piece.

To establish "Family Celebrations" we used the random factor that on a predetermined signal, everyone must stop and do a predetermined action. In their journal entries, many of the students had described attending weddings or large banquets with head tables. We used the idea of a head table for "Family Celebrations."

Students worked in small groups to create pieces using chairs in the following structure: Each individual selected a character for herself. She created a repeatable movement pattern that conveyed her personality, age, and relationship to the other people at the table. She could either use the movement pattern or sit and pretend to eat, drink, or chat with her neighbors. Everyone in the group sat at the head table except the photographer, who could walk out at any time and say, "Smile!," which was one of two predetermined signals. That would stop the action; everyone at the table would have to look front and smile, holding their positions for a given number of beats. The photographer could also stay offstage and call out, "Toast!" and each person at the table would have to clink her imaginary glass with the person closest to her and pretend to drink. To start the piece the photographer called out, "Smile!" several times, and the audience viewed a series of tableaux that showed a happy, convivial head table. A lot of humorous things happened after that. This piece requires little planning and rehearsal time and is great fun for theater students.

How We Used Wave Walk, Elastics, and Tag

Students were given cameras and tape recorders to capture sights and sounds for the "Rush Hour" and "Escapes" themes. We modified Wave Walk (see page 10) to re-create some aspects of rush hour crowds and used Elastics (see page 67) to connect people as they traveled around, over, and under each other while playing subway sounds the students had recorded. Just as in a real rush hour, things got tangled; movement became difficult and sometimes impossible. We also used variations on Onomatopoeia (see page 97), focusing on traffic and pedestrian sounds.

One of the movement pieces created for "Escapes" was a giant pinball machine, complete with sound effects. This was a very complex form of Tag (see page 14). There was a wonderful play between the students who were the balls

(they rolled, leaped, ran, and stumbled through the course) and the students who were the pins and obstacles (they lifted, spun, shook, and even sat on those who were the balls).

How We Used Recipes

Another way we explored the "Escapes" theme was with an ensemble dance recipe for a soloist and two groups of two or three. One of the groups represented the environment the soloist wants to escape from and the other the environment the soloist wants to escape to. The environments had to have contrasting qualities and work in different tempos. How the piece ended was up to each group. Some finished with the soloist in the environment she wanted to escape to, others had the soloist trapped in the environment she wanted to flee, and one group left the soloist in the middle, crouched on the floor, rocking back and forth, unable to move.

Here are some comments from the students who participated in the Urbanscape project that year:

- "Since the classes began I've been dancing at home. I haven't been feeling stressed out or worrying about things either . . . I always thought dance was symmetrical—you know, step by step, in sequence. Now I realize that dance can be anything you want it to be, even just walking down the street in rhythm."

- "Janice was excellent, she made sure everyone was involved and having fun. She didn't pressure you to be a dancer, but to dance, in your own way. We studied different aspects of the city that most of us take for granted or never even notice. This class made me aware of what's around me and the different movement patterns that are associated with it. This class is very worthwhile and advantageous to anyone who participates in it."

In the Urbanscape project students studied themselves, society, and their immediate environment. Their astute observations led to the creation of movement pieces of substance: choreography that expressed the students' sharp intelligence and sense of humor, their fears and frustrations, their hopes and dreams.

Movement and Computer Sciences: Dance Into the Picture

Step Into the Picture is a one-day, hands-on workshop that introduces high school students to the Adobe Photo Shop program. Created by Susan Middleton, a visual arts teacher and Through the Arts Studio coordinator at the Toronto Urban Studies Centre, this program has been running since 1993. I began working at the Centre in 1995, and in 1996 we piloted a three-day Dance Into the Picture program that introduced two ninth-grade classes from Danforth Collegiate and Technical Institute to the Photo Shop program, dance fundamentals, and visual and choreographic aesthetics.

To prepare, I attended several one-day Step Into the Picture workshops. Like many students participating in this workshop, I was a total novice at computer graphics. I was surprised and delighted at how quickly I was able to start getting results and how much fun the entire process was. Here is a brief outline of how Susan Middleton and the computer lab technicians run the one-day program.

Five stock photographic images are scanned into the computers for students to use for their initial exploration. The images consist of autumn leaves, ancient ruins, a sailboat, butterflies, and brightly painted gypsy wagons. Using one of the images, Susan and one of the computer technicians demonstrate how to view the images, select two of the five images in the computer to work with, and use a variety of filters and paint tools available in the menu that allow students to manipulate the images they have selected.

After this short demonstration students begin to work, one or two to a computer, for approximately 40 minutes. At that time Susan asks six to eight students to come into the neighboring studio for the next step: taking their own pictures. Students are shown how to operate digital cameras and work in pairs, taking pictures of their partners in various poses. When the first group finishes photographing, they return to the computer lab and send in the next group. This continues until everyone has been photographed. Then students are shown how to download their images into the computers.

After lunch there is a final demonstration that shows students how to select one of the photographs they have downloaded and put it into one of the stock pictures they manipulated with filters and paint tools in the morning session. The demonstration shows students how to use tools to cut out shapes, layer the shapes, and rotate or alter the perspective.

What amazed me was how similar this process was to creating dance. Manipulating and moving a photograph of myself through various twists and turns and placing it in different environments was armchair choreography. I felt that working with computers might be a great way to introduce shy nonmovers to the art of making dances.

Danforth Collegiate and Technical Institute's drama and visual arts teachers had approached the Toronto Urban Studies Centre about the possibility of having their ninth-grade students participate in a special integrated arts program. The majority of these students had had little arts exposure, especially in the area of dance. They were challenging classes, but the final product, in both movement and computer graphics, was successful.

Dance Into the Picture in Action

Our three-day program ran for consecutive Mondays. We worked with two classes simultaneously. Susan led the computer workshops while I worked in the dance studio next door. The first two days students spent two-and-a-half hours in the computer lab and two-and-a-half hours doing movement.

At the end of the first day students had learned how to select an image and manipulate it using filters and tools and had posed for five photographs taken with the digital cameras. They had learned a series of stretches and standing and across-the-floor dance combinations, were introduced to the general arts vocabulary, and used that vocabulary in discussions after performing Back to Front and Five Times Five.

Most of the students were timid movers, though a few were outstanding. In our discussions we reviewed the following terms: balance, texture, tone, repetition, rhythm, levels, direction, symmetry, and asymmetry.

The second Monday students manipulated their computer images into a finished product, keeping in mind the general arts vocabulary we had discussed the week before. In their half day with me they reviewed the stretches and movement combinations and performed and discussed Flocking and Wave Walk.

Their finished images were printed before their final visit (by the hardworking technicians in the computer lab), and we arranged the artwork on an oversized board so students could view the entire body of work. It was quite impressive.

After students viewed the art, we spent some time discussing it. I explained that I wanted to use the artwork as a foundation for creating movement pieces and asked the students to look at the artwork and identify any recurring images or patterns that we might be able to use as a theme in our movement work.

Multiple images were used in a number of pieces. Students had "cloned" themselves and had layered themselves or attached their bodies together to create larger shapes or lines that traveled through the picture. Though many of the images contained elements of unison and repetition, we agreed that the environments the bodies were placed in were very different and that this was a very important element. We discussed negative and positive space and how the images, colors, and textures in those spaces helped to communicate emotional environments. Another recurring element was magnifying or distorting one part of the body. We agreed that these exaggerated body parts gave the image a sense of direction and focus.

Circles and swirls formed by using the radial, twirl, and blur filters were also prevalent. Some students placed a single image of themselves at the center of the swirl. The textures and tones of the image outside the swirl varied. Some students had themselves in a colorful swirl while everything outside of that was gray. One student had himself in black and white staring out at a lush green world.

After a 20-minute stretch we began creating short movement pieces. Students worked in two large ensembles, and after a short discussion, both ensembles chose to use circular shapes as a foundation for the work. One group formed a large inward-facing circle. They changed levels, rocked from side to side, and froze in various shapes. Another group sat facing outward, reaching toward the viewers, drawing us in. We discussed the different qualities, then asked individuals to enter the circles to create a sense of inside versus outside.

One soloist started in the center of the circle. He escaped by pushing through and running out; another worked high levels within a low moving circle, creating a larger-than-life effect. In another group half of those in the circle slowly moved toward the center, creating a circle within a circle.

Everyone agreed that they had managed to communicate a number of the ideas and feelings expressed in the artwork. Not only had they created the swirls and circular shapes, they also emphasized body parts (reaching out to the

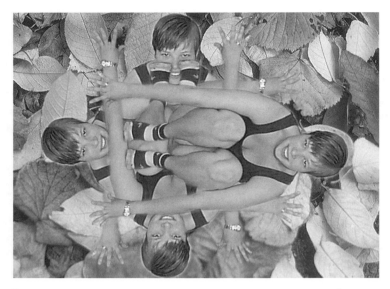

Leaves.

Architecture.

Butterflies. Artwork by Jessica McEwan.

audience) and unison and repetition (circles within circles). Each ensemble was able to communicate a distinctly different emotional environment. They had translated the color, tone, and textures used in their artwork into movement.

The accompanying artwork (next page) was created by Jessica McEwan, a grade 12 student, in May 2000 at the Toronto Urban Studies Centre. Teachers should note the way Jessica used the movement patterns in the stock photographs as inspiration for manipulating her own photo art. In the image of fall leaves, Jessica overlapped images of herself just as the leaves lie on top of each other. Jessica followed the architectural image by creating her own structure, using the same negative and positive pattern as in the building. For the image with butterflies, Jessica explored the idea of lightness (she, like the butterflies, hovers in the air) with her arm (distorted for more effect) and fingers spreading. Notice how her fingers echo the patterns in the butterflies' wings.

Movement, Music, and Visual Art: Art Through Art

In January 1991 the Art Gallery of Algoma, in Sault Sainte Marie, Ontario, hosted the first Art Through Art project for four classes of seventh- and eighth-grade students from district schools. The project had three main goals: to introduce students to the art gallery and its permanent collection of modern art, to offer students the opportunity to participate in movement and percussion classes, and to develop students' verbal and nonverbal communication skills.

The residency lasted two weeks, with each class attending five half-day sessions at the gallery. Each Monday students went on a tour of the gallery with Jane Coccimiglio, the gallery's education director. My partner, percussionist and composer Barry Prophet, and I accompanied the students and joined in the discussions. Following the tour we divided the class into two groups so that we could teach the movement and percussion workshops simultaneously in separate exhibition spaces.

Students worked for an hour in either movement or percussion, then switched rooms, so that everyone participated in both disciplines each day. Before students left that first day, they were given paper and pencils and asked to look at the artwork in the two main exhibition rooms one more time, then write down the title of the piece they found the most interesting. Barry, Jane, and I compiled the results. We used the students' two most favorite pieces as the foundation for the rest of the week's movement and music work. Compositions that the students created based on these pieces would be presented on the fifth and final day of the program.

Every day the students; their teachers; and Barry, Jane, and I participated in group discussions about the visual art. As planned, we focused on the pieces students had selected on the first day of the program. On Tuesday Jane asked students why they were attracted to the pieces they had selected, how the artwork made them feel, and what was the most interesting or eye-catching element in the work. During these discussions we were able to introduce terms such as tone, texture, rhythm, balance, line, attack, and harmony. After these discussions students went into their work groups and spent the next two hours doing percussion and movement exercises and learning how to apply the arts vocabulary to the sonic and physical realms.

By the third day students were using the terms quite comfortably. Working in the exhibition spaces with the paintings so close at hand helped students immeasurably. The artwork was concrete evidence of concepts students often have difficulty understanding. With a turn of the head they could see how lines can communicate different things. The thick, solid black grid of one painting contrasted brilliantly with a canvas covered in twisting pale blue and white lines and tiny glued-on swatches of blue and white cotton bedsheets. A giant canvas containing brightly colored symmetrical shapes perfectly illustrated aspects of balance, rhythm, and use of negative and positive space.

Art Through Art in Action

Students worked hard at interpreting the paintings, and even though they had limited skills in movement and music, each group created a short original piece that beautifully captured the essence of the artwork they were interpreting. We used variations on Wave Walk, Tag, and Flocking and dramatic gestures based on

Sound and Body Isolations to communicate emotional content and Body Bags, Bamboo Poles, and plastic and silk sheets to reproduce actual sections of the artwork.

The group of students that had selected the piece with the bold grid opened their piece by actually constructing a grid. One by one the students walked out and lay down on the floor to create a human grid. Once the grid was complete they used a static variation of Tag to allow each person an eight-beat solo. On the eighth beat the soloist touched the person to his right or left. No traveling movements were necessary because the bodies making up the grid were connected. By performing the solos on the spot the grid remained unbroken—exactly as in the painting.

When discussing their piece, one of the students in it said that they had to stay in place on the grid when they did their solos because "the grid was just like society with all of its rules and regulations. If you broke the rules, or got out of line, you got in trouble."

The group of students interpreting the same piece with Barry used a similar structure. The majority of the musicians played a strong 4/4 foundation while a smaller group of musicians played light and dark accents of chimes, rattles, and gongs.

Another group had selected the large canvas with the huge symmetrical shapes. Their piece started with everyone in the performance area frozen in shapes closely resembling those in the actual painting. Each shape was used by two people—some close to each other, some far away—but the overall effect was very balanced. They began the movement very slowly, using skills they had developed from Mirroring and Flocking and then allowed each pair a fast, dynamic action (jump, leap, roll) followed by a freeze. The piece ended as it had begun—with pairs of symmetrical shapes frozen throughout the space.

The musicians also used pairings. The piece was made up of small duets that were strung together by a group of foundation players. In both of these classes students commented on how well the music and the movement complemented each other. If we had had just a little more time with the students, we would have arranged the music and the dance so that they could have been performed together.

In five half-day gallery visits students had accomplished a tremendous amount. From having little or no arts exposure, most students were able to speak clearly and confidently about the artwork in the gallery and the movement and music pieces they had created. They had worked cooperatively throughout the program and had developed problem-solving skills and rehearsal discipline. Their teachers were impressed with the seriousness and honesty that so many of them brought to the project. The parents who were able to attend the presentations (they were held during regular working hours) commented on how enthusiastic their children had been throughout the week of classes.

Here are some comments from students who attended the classes that year:

- "When I first came into your class I thought you were out of it, but as we got further in your classes I found you were neat. Your classes made me feel like I was in a dream world; I wouldn't change anything. If I had the chance I'd do it again."

- "The first day I went to the Art Gallery I found what we were doing very strange: moving up and down in different shapes, making contrasts and funny sounds. I felt embarrassed until I noticed that everybody was doing the same things as me. I found our discussions [about the art] very interesting in the way we got our minds thinking. Some of the ideas that people came up with were very brilliant. By the end of the week when the music and movement were put together they really gave insight into the paintings. When it came time to leave I didn't want to go. Now I plan to visit the Art Gallery more often. I really had fun."

While Art Through Art was in progress, Sault Sainte Marie was hosting the International Winter Cities Conference. This international conference gives northern communities from around the world a chance to meet and share their ideas and concerns about the unique challenges facing those living in northern climates. The Art Gallery of Algoma, like many other art, theater, and exhibition spaces in the north, is always busy during the tourist season, but in the winter months it is used less frequently by the local community. During Art Through Art the gallery was hopping! The project succeeded in combining resources (artists, educators, artwork, exhibition spaces) for the benefit of the community (students, teachers, parents) and provided an exceptional introductory arts education program that could not be offered in a school setting or at the gallery during the busy summer months. Art Through Art was so enthusiastically received that Barry and I returned in the fall of 1995 to repeat the program for a whole new group of seventh- and eighth-grade students.

More Comments

Students, educators, and parents comment on opportunities for growth experienced while working in creative choreographic projects.

- "The students were engaged the moment they met her. She [Janice] provided them with the opportunity to explore their own limits as they stretched and explored variations of movement structures. . . . It was an opportunity for students to not only focus on developing their creativity, but also develop problem-solving, decision-making, cooperative-learning, and discipline skills so necessary for the well-rounded individual." —Elementary school vice-principal

- "Since we, the students, were given the opportunity to do the choreography ourselves, the responsibility was given to us to take risks. The final product makes me proud to be a part of this creative movement piece. If any one person hadn't contributed what they did, the final product would not have been as successful." —Grade 8 student

- "I learned to work with a big group of people, to handle complications, experiment more, deal with struggles, conflict, and accept more ideas." —Grade 8 student

- "My group had to overcome a few problems. One big one was that when we were choreographing we could never agree on what to do. Half of us would want to use a step that the other half didn't like or couldn't do. We struggled through though, and either changed the step to something everyone liked or the people who couldn't do the step worked really hard to learn how." —Grade 8 student

- "As our son's grade 7 year comes to an end we look back on this experience as one of the ones that expanded his horizons and encouraged him to try creative movement and interpretation, photography and integration of music—all artistic explorations to which he would not otherwise be exposed. It was remarkable to us that these classes brought out forms of expression in him that we had never seen before. Without this program he would have remained a shyer young man." —Parents of Grade 7 student

- "My son attended this program with his teacher and other members of his grade 7 class. I was fortunate to have viewed the final presentation. I saw students writing and presenting their own group poetry, closely choreographed works to music, fabulous nature slides taken by the students themselves and reshaped into performance pieces. The work was joyful, multidisciplinary, and intense." —Parent of Grade 7 student

Random Factor Variations

*F*ollowing is a list of the random factor variations used in the exercises, along with the page number that they appear on.

Chapter One: Rules

- Physically connect to another person. (page 5)
- Make the frozen shapes move. (page 8)
- Overlap two ensembles. (page 13)
- Incorporate neutral bodies into the exercise. (page 16)
- Try to do everything at once. (page 18)
- Change the spatial relationships in the exercise. (page 21)
- Combine two exercises. (page 24)
- Interact with another without touching. (page 27)
- Use movement vocabulary from an everyday activity. (page 29)
- Keep one part of your body frozen while the rest moves. (page 31)
- Emphasize contrasting movements. (page 33)
- Ring a bell for freedom. (page 35)

Chapter Two: Recipes

- Change the quality of the action. (page 40)
- Have the audience watch from all sides. (page 41)
- Change all aspects of the timing. (page 42)
- Change the number of participants. (page 45)
- Change the size of the performance area. (page 47)
- Emphasize a specific body part. (page 48)
- Add a hula hoop. (page 50)
- Reverse the order. (page 52)

- Work in total silence. (page 54)
- Change the ending. (page 56)
- Explore environmental sounds. (page 59)

Chapter Three: Props

- Communicate an emotion. (page 64)
- Create your own sounds. (page 65)
- Move under, over, and around the exercise. (page 68)
- Tell a story. (page 71)
- Work with only half the number of costumes or props. (page 74)
- Explore a contrasting vocabulary. (page 77)
- Become the object you are moving. (page 80)

Chapter Four: Poetry and Prose

- Turn the movement into a canon (round). (page 87)
- Create a dance map. (page 90)
- Create your own recipe. (page 92)
- Combine two random factor variations. (page 95)
- Combine three contrasting sounds. (page 98)
- Have everyone perform the exercise while holding different props. (page 100)
- Eliminate the use of verbs and arm movements. (page 103)
- Create a sonic collage. (page 105)
- Create your own random factor variation. (page 108)

Chapter Five: Objects and Images

- Change the performance area so that it takes on the appearance of a game board. (page 114)
- Have one movement pattern overwhelm and transform another. (page 119)
- Create a 12- to 24-beat movement phrase that can be repeated five different ways. (page 120)
- Maintain only half the required shape. (page 124)
- Create new ensembles by mixing members from contrasting ensembles. (page 126)
- Turn off the overhead lights and use handheld flashlights to illuminate the movement, or set spotlights to illuminate certain areas the movements pass through. (page 128)
- Project slides or hand-painted transparencies on students' work. (page 131)
- Create a costume that turns part of the body into a piece of art. (page 133)

Following are lists of additional random factor variations.

Variations That Focus on Manipulating the Shape or Action of the Movers

- Animate the knees and elbows.
- Change the footwork to contrast with the rest of the body.
- Keep one hand on the floor at all times.
- Present the exercise with participants facing any direction but front.
- Limit movements and shapes to those found in sports.
- Explore drawing figure-eights with arms, legs, and torso while traveling across the floor.
- Make the entire exercise asymmetrical.
- Make the entire exercise symmetrical.
- Remove several of the required elements or steps and replace them with your own ideas.
- Change the original starting shape of the exercise (e.g., explore ways to do Back to Front in a circle).
- Try to work on as many levels as possible (e.g., instead of walking, participants may do low rolls, knee work, or leaps).
- See what happens when half the performers work in the original order while the other half work in reverse.
- Predetermine a specific sound cue that signals participants to jump four times, roll on the ground, dust themselves, and then continue the original exercise.
- Have someone recite the multiplication tables while others perform.
- Have some students read newspapers or magazines aloud.

Variations That Affect the Performance Area

- Have the audience travel around the performers while the performers work in a central spot.
- Perform the exercise as if working on a sticky floor.
- Perform the exercise as if the Earth's gravity has changed to that of the moon.
- Perform the exercise as if you were walking on eggshells.
- Perform the exercise as if crossing a ship's deck during a storm.
- If you have access to risers (stage platforms), use them to create at least three different levels throughout the performance space.
- Scatter newspapers or magazines across the floor. Performers must not touch them while they work.
- Do the exercise in a classroom and incorporate all of the desks and chairs.
- Perform the exercise in a busy hallway or foyer.

Variations That Require Costumes and Props

- Wear masks: neutral masks, traditional masks from a variety of cultures, masks made from paper bags, handheld masks, and so on.
- Have everyone pretend to chew gum in an exaggerated fashion as they perform the exercise.
- Work in the darkness with movers holding lit sparklers.
- Put on skates (ice or in-line) and perform outdoors.
- Have one, two, or three people dribble a ball while others perform a slow-moving or lyrical movement exercise.
- Cover the floor with fabric and perform the exercise under the fabric.

Variations Using Different Timings and Emotions

- Perform the exercise using extreme timings (work as slowly or as quickly as possible).
- Perform the exercise with variable timings (assign different speeds to individuals and see what happens when contrasting speeds work side by side).
- Frequently change the timing of the exercise (ring a bell every 30 seconds to signal a change from fast to slow or from slow to fast).
- Explore different time signatures. Most North American popular and European classical music is in 4/4 or 3/4 time (or variations of it, e.g., 2/4 or 6/8). If you are not familiar with other timings, use the discography included in appendix C and start listening to world music. Quite a lot of Middle Eastern, African, Asian, and Indo-Pacific music is not in 4/4 or 3/4. Try creating or re-creating movement phrases to 5/4 timing. You may find it hard to count 1, 2, 3, 4, 5; 1, 2, 3, 4, 5 because you have grown accustomed to always starting over at 3 or 4. A simple way to count 5/4 timing is 1, 2, 3, 1, 2; 1, 2, 3, 1, 2. Make sure you give equal time value to each beat.
- Select two contrasting emotions and have participants start an exercise communicating one emotion, then shifting into the second emotion midway through it. Can the shift occur seamlessly, or does there need to be a signal or stimulus to cause the shift in mood?
- Combine contrasting music and emotions. Try performing a slow, grief-filled movement phrase to fast, upbeat music. A simple way to do this is to try Flocking to music with a quick, driving pulse. Make sure half the class watches while the others do the exercise. After everyone has watched and performed, discuss the outcome. Sometimes selecting a contrasting music can create a powerful image. Why does that happen? When can this concept be used?

Warm-Up Ideas

*T*he following warm-up ideas are for students and teachers with little or no movement experience.

It is important to develop students' strength, flexibility, and body awareness as they explore the creative movement process. The more physically confident a student becomes, the less likely he is to be inhibited or intimidated by the movement exercises in this book. As the students' physical skills develop, so will their ability to express themselves with greater physical clarity and control. Movement skills that are introduced in the warm-up are reinforced in the creative work. Similarly, an idea inspired through creative work may challenge students to develop greater technical skills.

If you are working in an elementary school and have only 45 to 60 minutes to teach your movement or physical education class, you should develop a 10- to 15-minute warm-up that physically and mentally focuses your students. A 3- to 4-minute cardiovascular wake-up is a great way to start.

Wake Up

Make sure everyone is wearing proper footwear (no hard-soled shoes) or is barefoot. Have students walk or run as quickly and quietly as possible throughout the room (I like to discourage students from walking around and around in a circle by asking them to touch the four walls or corners in as short a time as possible). Students should be encouraged to follow their own path and to move through spaces where no one else is traveling. Once that method of moving has been established, ask students to move throughout the room while responding to a variety of tempo and direction changes. Try calling out the following: "walk sideways," "take tiny steps," "walk backward," "take uneven steps," "freeze," "fall to the floor," "rise up," "hop on one foot," and so on. Keep this going for about three minutes and finish off with 30 to 60 seconds (depending on the students' stamina) of fast running on the spot. Have students keep their spines long and stretch their arms out in front of them at waist height. While they are "running" they should lift their legs high enough that their knees touch their hands.

Stretches

Now that the mind and body are awake and the muscles are warm, spend five to six minutes doing floor stretches. The following stretches focus primarily on lengthening the spine, releasing tension in the back of the neck and lower back, and stretching and strengthening the hamstrings and inside thigh muscles.

Have students sit on the floor, all facing the same direction. Ask them to sit with their spines straight, their legs in front with knees bent (pointing out to the sides), and the soles of their feet pressed together approximately one foot away from the torso, so that their feet and legs form a diamond shape on the floor in front of them. People have a tendency to place their hands on their feet when they are in this position, but doing so causes the spine to tilt forward. Instead, leave the arms relaxed at either side. Once everyone is ready to start, ask the students to drop their heads and slowly lengthen the spine so that the head hangs down toward the feet. As the torso lowers, their arms will extend out to the sides, and the shoulder blades will relax and open to either side as the spine lengthens and lowers.

Those who are flexible should have no trouble getting the tops of their heads to touch their feet. Have them remain in that position for 8 to 16 beats so that the lower and middle back gets a good stretch. Then slowly roll back up, reversing the spinal roll so that the head lifts up last. This is very important as it prevents the back of the neck from arching backward. You may wish to try this sequence with the following counts: 8 counts to roll down through the spine, 16 counts to hold, 8 counts to roll back up; then 4 counts to roll down, 8 counts to hold, 4 back up; finally, 2 counts to roll down, 4 counts to hold, 2 counts up.

Make sure students start and finish each sequence with a tall, straight spine (I like to tell students to imagine that the tops of their heads are being pulled up gently toward the ceiling) and that they breathe deeply and keep their heads down for all of the counts in the stretched-spine position.

Do the same roll and stretch count sequences in the following positions:

- With one leg stretched straight out in front while the other remains in the original bent position so that the foot of the bent leg is touching inside the knee of the straightened leg (repeat with opposite leg outstretched).

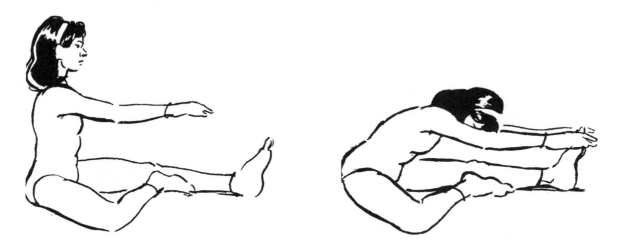

- With both legs stretched straight out in front, hip-width (or a minimum of six inches) apart, knees straight, feet flexed (soles of feet pressed forward, toes toward the ceiling). Instead of trying to get the head to touch the feet (which are now too far away), students should try to lengthen their spines a bit so that the tops of their heads go beyond their knees. This stretch is difficult for those who have short, tight hamstrings. Those students may experience discomfort in the back of the neck, across the upper back and shoulder blade area, and all along the back of the legs. Students who experience pain while attempting this stretch should be allowed to bend their knees slightly. Make sure that the knees point up toward the ceiling as opposed to out to the sides, and that students keep their feet flexed and head down while in the stretch position.

● With legs extended out to the sides in a wide *V.* In this position it is important not to let the legs roll in. Make sure that the knees remain facing the ceiling, especially when the spine rolls down and the top of the head reaches toward or touches the floor. To prevent the legs and feet from rolling in, students must think of lengthening and strengthening their inside thigh muscles. Feet can be pointed or flexed. Flexed is more challenging, as it increases the hamstring stretch.

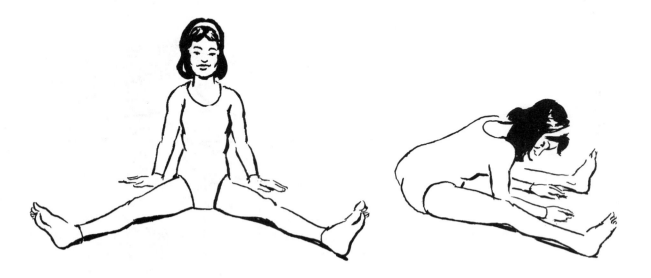

There are lots of other floor stretches you can do. Experiment on your own, or ask students to offer suggestions. Remind them that when stretching they must always remember to breathe. Holding the breath inhibits the muscles' natural ability to lengthen and release.

Abdominal Strengthening

Always do some lower abdominal strengthening exercises such as curl-ups (similar to sit-ups and described in the next paragraph as part of the stretching regimen).

Have students lie with their backs on the floor, legs hip-width (minimum six inches) apart, knees bent up toward the ceiling, feet flat on the floor. Hands should be placed lightly on the thighs, palms down. On the count of 1 carefully lift the head from the floor and place the chin on the chest. On the count of 2 stretch the arms out and up along the legs, lengthening the fingers and reaching out beyond the knees. This arm action will bring the shoulders up off the floor. It all happens smoothly and quickly on one beat. Hold this position for counts 3, 4, 5, 6, 7, 8, 9, and 10. Make sure that the chin stays down on the chest. This lengthens the back of the neck and prevents the weight of the head from pulling the neck back and into an arch. Roll back down to the starting position for counts 11 and 12. Repeat this 5 to 10 times. Remind students that this is not a full-blown sit-up. Only the head, neck, and shoulders are lifted off the floor. Students should feel the lower abdominal muscles working as the head, neck, and shoulders curl up, and even more so while they maintain the hold. Remind people to keep breathing by calling out the counts as follows: "One, inhale, bring the chin to your chest; two, lengthen your arms, reach through your fingers as your shoulders lift off the floor; exhale as you hold the position, three, four, five, six; stay there as you inhale, seven, eight, nine, ten; exhale deeply as you relax and carefully lower the arms, upper body, neck, and head, eleven, twelve."

Lower abdominal awareness and strength is one of the basic requirements for controlling balance. Experiment with the following balancing variations.

Balancing

Start with everyone standing in neutral position: feet and legs hip-width apart, toes straight ahead, knees straight (but not locked), hips and shoulders squarely front, spine and neck long and tall, eyes focused to the front. Remind students to be aware of their lower abdominal muscles. One way to do this is to have students imagine a line or chain that gently pulls the navel to the spine. Bend both knees slightly, then slowly straighten the legs and feel the weight of the body shift slightly onto the front of the feet. Then imagine the top of the head lengthening up to the ceiling. As the head lengthens up, the torso, legs, and feet will follow the movement upward and the heels will lift off of the floor. This way the whole body is involved in the lift, not just the feet. Continue to lift the heels and work through the arches until only the balls of the feet and the toes are on the floor. Breathe and hold for four counts, then slowly lengthen the body downward and lower the heels to the floor. Always work gently and carefully through the feet. Repeat the sequence, this time holding the balance for eight counts. Repeat a third time and allow students to remain balancing with their heels lifted off the floor for as long as possible. Throughout this sequence the arms should remain at the sides or stretched out to either side at shoulder height.

Balancing requires the entire body to be active. Engage the lower abdominal muscles to prevent the torso from wiggling. Always remind students to think of lengthening the tops of their heads toward the ceiling. This will help them lift the body's weight up out of their hips. Do not let the students lift the shoulders as they rise; instead, have them gently pull the shoulder blades down the back so that the shoulders and the hips stay connected, the torso solid. This will help the body maintain the alignment required for balance.

More Balances

Try balancing on one leg. Start off bending the knees as before, but instead of straightening both legs, slowly straighten one leg while simultaneously lifting the other foot off the ground, as if stepping up a stair. Continue to straighten the "standing" leg, then let the heel of the "standing" leg lift slightly off the ground. Hold the balance for as long as possible, then gently lower to the starting position. Repeat, alternating legs.

Finish this segment with balances where the entire foot of the standing leg stays planted on the ground. Try balances that focus on changing the position of the lifted leg. You can stretch the lifted leg to the front, side, or back. The lifted leg can be straight or bent, turned out or parallel. Have students experiment with balances and present their findings to each other. Students may explore variations of the spine and arms as well as the legs. Do not let them attempt balances such as headstands or handstands without partners or mats. Ask qualified physical education teachers for assistance when introducing these movements to the students.

Across the Floor

Have students jump, skip, leap, hop, and run across the floor two or three at a time. If neither you nor your students have training in across-the-floor dance combinations, try the simple movement patterns listed below.

Have students try the following across-the-floor patterns:

- Jump four times on the spot, then run forward for four counts; jump four times on the spot, run forward for four counts. Repeat until you get to the other side of the room.

- Hop forward two times on the right foot, then hop forward two times on the left foot. Continue smoothly alternating the hops from right foot to left foot until you get to the other side of the room.

- Run forward for three counts and then leap off of one foot and land on the other. Repeat until you get to the other side.

- Try running backward. For safety, position some students at the far side of the room to catch the runners before they collide with the wall. Students must use focus and peripheral vision when moving backward. Ask them to focus on a spot on the wall they are moving away from and to stay in line with that spot as they move away from it. At the same time, students must use their peripheral vision to maintain awareness of those running beside them. (Practicing the Wave Walk, in chapter 1, helps students develop their peripheral vision.)

- Do a low-level roll for four counts, take two counts to stand, then take two counts to go back down to the floor. Repeat the roll, standing, and returning to the floor.

Final Note

A 10- to 15-minute warm-up cannot take the place of technique-based movement classes. As your students' strength and confidence increase, try introducing some dance technique, mime, and stage fighting classes into your program. If you do not feel that you are able to lead these classes, consider contacting local dance and theater companies for the names of professional guest artists who can come to your school.

Through regular stretching and strengthening and cardiovascular warm-ups, students develop an understanding of their physical abilities and limitations. This knowledge helps them develop awareness of their own bodies along with respect for the abilities and limitations of others.

Discography

*T*hese are just a few of the recordings I like to use with my students. Exposure to a wide range of music helps students develop mature movement and music aesthetics.

Musical albums are listed by title, artist, and recording company, followed by letters denoting these classifications: M (meditative), O (orchestral), P (percussion), S (string), ST (soundtrack), V (vocal), WMC (world music contemporary), WMJ (world music jazz), and WMT (world music traditional).

11,000 Virgins, Chants for the Feast of St. Ursula, Anonymous 4, Harmonia Mundi (M, V)

A Circle is Cast, Libana, Spinning Records (M, V)

A Sublime Trance, Pt. Shiv Kumar Sharma, Immortal Series (M, WMT)

Adventures in Afropea 1, Zap Mama, Crammed Discs (V, WMC)

Ambient Music for Airports, Brian Eno, EG Records (M)

American Composers Orchestra 1, Harrison/Ung/McPhee, Argo (O)

Apocalypse Now Sessions, Mickey Hart and the Rhythm Devils, Rykodisc (P, ST)

Ask Me No Questions, Djivan Gasparyan, Crossroads CD (M, WMT)

Bar Kokhba, John Zorn and Masada Chamber Ensemble, Hips Records (WMJ)

Best of Both Worlds, 2 CD sampler, Rykodisc & Hannibal's World (WMC/J/T)

The Chieftains Collection, The Chieftains, Claddagh Records (WMT)

Chinese Traditional Pipa Music, Liu Fang, Oliver Sudden Productions (S, WMT)

Cor, Maria Joao, Verve (V)

Crystal Bones, Barry Prophet and Janice Pomer, Inde (P)

Dolmen Music, Meredith Monk, ECM New Series (V)

Drumming, Steve Reich, Elektra/Nonesuch (P)

Drums for Tomorrow, Amampondo, M.E.L.T. 2000 (P)

Drums of Passion, Olatunji, Columbia (P)

The Essential Oregon, Oregon, Vanguard (WMC/J)

In C, Terry Riley, Shanghai Film Orchestra, Celestial Harmonies (O)

Karelia Visa, Hedningarna, Northside (WMC)

Koyaanisqatsi, Philip Glass, Island Masters (ST)

L.A.G.Q., Los Angles Guitar Quartet, Sony (S)

Laya Vinya, Trichy Sankaran, Music of the World (WMT)

The Minimalists, performed by the London Chamber Orchestra, Virgin Classics (O)

Music of Nias & North Sumatra, Smithsonian Folkways (WMT)

New Ancient Strings, Toumani Diabate, Hannibal's World (WMT)

Nordan, Lena Willemark & Ale Moller, ECM (WMC)

Opus 1, Pan African Orchestra, Real World (WMC/T)

Pieces of Africa, Kronos Quartet, Elecktra Nonesuch (S)

Ragas & Sagas, Jan Garbarek and Ustad Fateh Ali Khan, ECM (WMJ)

Score from The Catherine Wheel, David Byrne, Sire Records (ST)

Show of Hands, Robert Fripp and The League of Crafty Guitarists, EG Music Inc. (S)

Spirit of the Forest, Baka Beyond, Rykodisc (WMC)

Talking Timbukta, Ali Farka Toure and Ry Cooder, Rykodisc (WMC)

Tarab, Rabih Abou Khalil, enja (WMJ)

Towards the Rising Sun, Ravi Shankar and Friends, Deutsch Gramophone (WMT)

appendix

D

Assessment Strategies

*A*ssessment strategies go in and out of fashion as school curricula change. Educational curricula differ from province to province, state to state, and country to country. It would be impossible for me to address all of the current assessment strategies used by teachers reading this book, so instead I will outline a simple structure that teachers can adapt to a variety of systems.

The structure divides students' work into two areas: Individual (the work students do that they are solely responsible for) and Ensemble (the work students do as class members and in small ensembles), and each of those areas has two subsections. (Please note the skills I look for are listed alphabetically.) I have used this system for 20 years whenever I do an extended dance project in the schools and teachers ask me to assess the students' creative movement work.

Individual/Creative (25% of full mark)

- ability to explore new ways of moving
- creative use of technical movement skills
- development of performance dynamics
- development of personal aesthetics in solo choreography
- level of focus and concentration
- personal journal entries (when applicable)
- willingness to challenge oneself physically and mentally
- willingness to contribute ideas in the discussion section
- willingness to take creative risks

Individual/Technical (25% of full mark)

- ability to create challenging shapes
- ability to listen to and follow instructions
- ability to perform specific movement sequences

- awareness of body alignment
- commitment to performing an exercise to the best of one's ability
- coordination of fine and gross motor skills
- flexibility
- musicality
- physical strength

Ensemble/Process (25% of full mark)

- ability to contribute ideas and listen to others when working in a group
- ability to rehearse choreography with others
- awareness of others' needs (space) when working in large group
- considerate of others' technical abilities (weaknesses and strengths)
- creative use of technical movement skills
- leadership skills
- supports others' ideas when working in ensembles
- supports others physically when working in large group and ensembles
- uses ensemble etiquette while planning choreography
- uses problem-solving skills when working in large group and ensembles
- willingness to work with all members of the class (not just friends)

Product (25% of full mark)

- ability to follow the assignment's structure
- ability to take risks in a performance setting
- ability to translate concrete information into dance
- commitment to the work as one performs it
- dramatic expression and performance dynamics
- generosity of spirit on stage (especially when things don't go as planned)
- quality of product presented (be it a "work in progress" or rehearsed choreography)
- use of improvisational problem-solving skills when things don't go as planned

With this approach teachers can do daily assessment or use the presentation of exercises and choreographic assignments as benchmarks. Teachers can add or subtract skills students are assessed on and assign percentage values as they see fit.

Stage Picture

I use stage directions all the time. Once students are familiar with them, stage directions simplify speaking and writing out choreographic directions. The stage is divided into nine stage areas. Imagine drawing a giant tic-tac-toe grid across the stage. That is exactly how the stage area is divided. Read the description below for better understanding of the nine stage areas and specific terminology.

Practice giving stage directions. Have students practice moving to the directions. Use the examples given and make up some of your own.

Length

The three equal areas for stage length are as follows:

- Downstage: The third of the stage that is closest to the audience.
- Upstage: The third of the stage that is farthest away from the audience.
- Center stage: The third of the stage that runs between downstage and upstage.

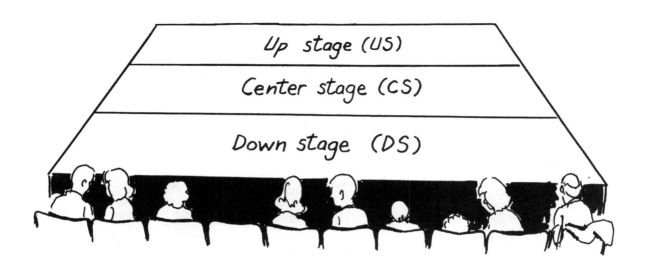

Depth

The three equal areas for stage depth are as follow:

- Stage right: The third of the stage that the audience views as its left.
- Stage left: The third of the stage that the audience views as its right.
- Center stage: The third of the stage that runs between stage right and stage left.

(Remember: Stage directions are for the performers on stage. That is why it seems as if stage right and stage left are reversed.)

Combine the two areas to give clear, easy-to-follow stage directions: "The person who is upstage right, please roll slowly to downstage left"; "Let's have center stage right and center stage left exchange places with stage right, moving downstage slightly to avoid collision."

You can use abbreviations to save time (this is great for taking notes): "DSR grp. arrive CS in 9 beats. Jen enters USL, Chris enters USR."

Glossary of Movement Terms

*T*his movement vocabulary can be applied to all art forms; dancers and nondancers alike find them very user-friendly. Communication is intrinsic to the arts. It is imperative, then, that students and teachers share a vocabulary that enables them to express their ideas, emotions, and personal aesthetics clearly to one another.

In this general vocabulary I refer to visual, emotional, and sonic elements. Dance contains all of these elements: visual dynamics (the dancers and the choreography), the emotional content built into the choreography (subtext), and sonics (music, voice, breath, or beat of footsteps). The word audience refers to the person(s) viewing or listening to the art.

action—Something that physically or emotionally moves the performer(s), the audience, or both.

attack—The weight, speed, or pressure behind an action, or a combination of these. The method of approaching a visual, emotional, or sonic element.

asymmetry—An individual or group shape that is not the same on both sides (see **symmetry**).

balance—Harmony of any or all visual, emotional, or sonic elements.

beat—A single moment in time, or a series of accented images, feelings, or sounds.

color—A distinct visual, emotional, or sonic element that communicates a specific mood.

direction—A pathway of movement (e.g., straight, diagonal, circular, random). A place for individuals or a group to face or move away from (see **external focus** and **internal focus**).

discord—Clashing or conflicting visual, emotional, or sonic elements or any combination of these.

dynamics—Range of expression (e.g., fast to slow, loud to soft, emotional diversity, high to low levels).

external focus—Direction in which individuals or a group look, move toward, or both. The direction or place that the audience's eyes are drawn to.

external neutral—A physical position with spine held straight, shoulders over hips, hips over knees, knees over feet, and toes facing front.

harmony—When visual, emotional, or sonic elements, or any combination of these, complement each other.

internal focus—Concentration of all mental and physical energy to an action or stillness.

internal neutral—A position for face, mind, and body that communicates as little emotion as possible.

levels—High, medium, and low heights and the increments in between. Also, application of these heights to create shapes or movement patterns that incorporate a range of height and depth.

line—A series of sounds, images, actions, or feelings, or any combination of these, that may or may not be physically connected but have direction or communicate a specific idea or emotional state.

motion—An action that travels through the body; an action that is used to travel across the room or performance space.

pattern—A visual, emotional, or sonic form that may or may not be repeated but is repeatable.

quality—A distinctive characteristic of a visual, emotional, or sonic element.

resonance—The length of time that a visual, emotional, or sonic element sustains itself in the eyes, minds, or ears of the audience.

rhythm—A measured flow of sound, action, or both.

sequence—A running order of movement, sonic, or text-based phrases.

shape—Forms individuals or groups create while performing an action or holding a freeze.

space—The distance between individuals, or the performance area itself.

symmetry—Individual or group shape that is the same on both sides, creating a mirror image.

texture—The quality or distinctive feel of a visual, emotional, or sonic element.

time—How we measure our existence (past, present, and future); the duration of a solitary action or sound or a combination of actions and sounds.

tone—The shade or character of a visual, emotional, or sonic element (see **color**).

weight—The emotional or physical force used in an action or sound.

About the Author

Janice Pomer has been teaching and performing in the fields of dance, theatre, and music since 1976. She has been a guest artist in schools, universities, international education conferences, dance studios, and art centers in communities throughout North America and has been awarded numerous grants in support of her innovative education and performance work from the Ontario Arts Council. Janice has introduced thousands of elementary and high school students to creative movement and choreography in a variety of special projects that integrate dance with visual art, music, theatre, architecture, nature, and urban studies. She has taught and created programs for the Canadian Children's Dance Theatre (1983-1995), the National Ballet of Canada's education department (1990-1997), the Children's Dance Project (1993-2000), and the Toronto Urban Studies Centre, Through the Arts Studio (1996-2001). Janice teaches modern dance at Pegasus Children's Dance Centre in Toronto, Ontario, Canada. She can be reached by e-mail at **jpomer@look.ca**.